Letterland

Early Years Handbook

Published by Letterland International Ltd.
8/10 South Street, Epsom, Surrey, KT18 7PF, UK

www.letterland.com

ISBN: 978-1-86209-226-6
Product Code: EYH

First published by Letterland Ltd 1995
New edition published 1997 by Collins Educational, reprinted 1999.
Revised edition published 2003. Reprinted 2006, 2007, 2008.
This revised edition published 2011. Reprinted 2013, 2014, 2018, 2020, 2021.
LETTERLAND™ is a trademark of Letterland International Ltd.

Judy Manson and Mark Wendon assert the moral right to be identified as the authors of this work.

British Library Cataloguing in Publication Data
A catalogue record for this book is available from the British Library.

Photographs by Martin Sookias, Steve Lumb & Janine Hosegood
Design by Sally Boothroyd and Susi Martin
Cover design by Susi Martin
Pictogram artwork by Geri Livingston
Printed in Singapore

Acknowledgments
The authors and publishers would like to thank the following:
The staff and children at Allfarthing Primary School, Earlsfield; London Caterpillar Nursery, Balham, London; Charlbury Primary School, Charlbury, Oxfordshire; Flora Garden School, Hammersmith, London and St Wilfred's Nursery School, Burgess Hill for their help with the photographs
Sue Leverton for her teaching advice

Letterland

Early Years Handbook

by Judy Manson and Mark Wendon

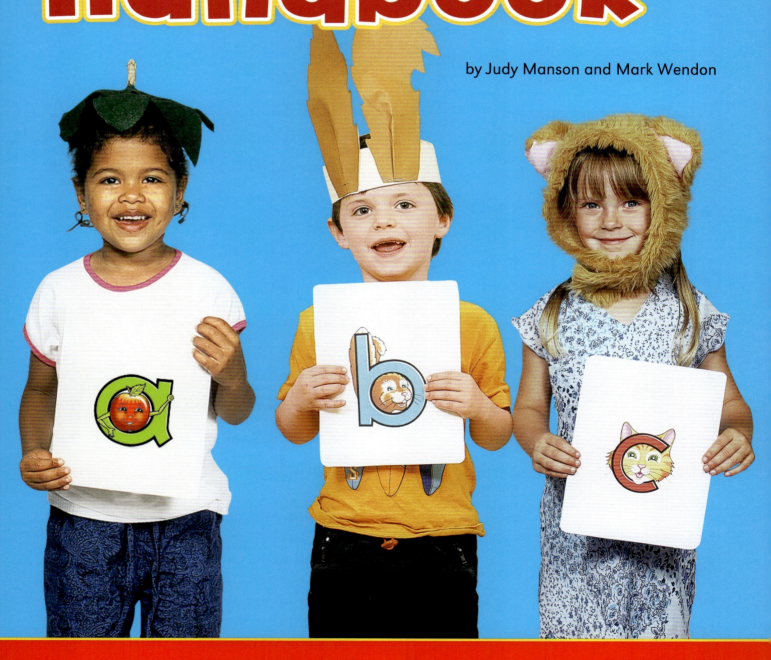

Early literacy skills

Contents

Foreword 5

Introduction to Letterland 6

Who is Letterland for? 7

The Early Years Programme 8

    The materials 8

    Notes about the materials 8-11

Teaching with Letterland 12

    The 'journey to Letterland' 12

    Teaching each alphabet letter 12

    Letter shapes 13

    Letter names and sounds 14

    Capital letters 14

    Long vowels 15

    Parental involvement 15

    Your own ideas 15

Further ideas 16-19

Aa: Annie Apple 20

Bb: Bouncy Ben 22

Cc: Clever Cat 24

Dd: Dippy Duck 26

Ee: Eddy Elephant 28

Ff: Firefighter Fred 30

Gg: Golden Girl 32

Hh: Harry Hat Man 34

Ii: Impy Ink 36

Jj: Jumping Jim 38

Kk: Kicking King 40

Ll: Lucy Lamp Light 42

Mm: Munching Mike 44

Nn: Noisy Nick 46

Oo: Oscar Orange 48

Pp: Peter Puppy 50

Qq: Quarrelsome Queen 52

Rr: Red Robot 54

Ss: Sammy Snake 56

Tt: Talking Tess 58

Uu: Uppy Umbrella 60

Vv: Vicky Violet 62

Ww: Walter Walrus 64

Xx: Fix-it Max 66

Yy: Yellow Yo-yo Man 68

Zz: Zig Zag Zebra 70

The Alphabet Songs 72-75

The Handwriting Songs 76-77

The Actions Trick 78-79

Letter to parents 80

Early Years Foundation Stage Abbreviations

Personal, Social and Emotional (PSE)
Communication, Language and Literacy (CLL)
Problem Solving, Reasoning and Numeracy (PSRN
Knowledge and Understanding of the World (KU)
Physical Development (PD)
Creative Development (CD)

Foreword

Children love to be told stories, and listen to them simply because they want to! In devising the Letterland system, I took full advantage of this by transforming the dry language of phonics instruction into a series of fun phonics fables, full of alliteration and anecdotes. These stories uniquely bring the facts to life, and children as young as three – as well as older children of all abilities, including children with learning difficulties – soon latch on to them. They find it easy to remember, for example, that Harry Hat Man hates noise because it gives him a **h**orrible **h**eadache, so when he's in a word he never speaks above a whisper. He just says, '**hhh**!'

By combining phonics teaching with storytelling, Letterland aims to provide an appealing way to teach letter shape and sound recognition, and to establish correct letter formation, while at the same time engendering a delight in language and learning. Used in pre-schools and nurseries, it lays the foundations for reading, writing and spelling so engagingly that the children cannot distinguish it from play and their favourite story times. Furthermore it addresses many of the Early Years Foundation Stage learning objectives along the way. So enjoy being the children's travel guide as you take them on a journey through Letterland!

Lyn

Introduction to Letterland

Many thousands of children have learnt to read and write with Letterland. This Handbook is primarily designed to help Early Years practitioners use the unique Letterland system in nurseries and pre-schools. It can also be used with school age children in settings where teachers prefer **a-z** learning to start at Primary School. This book's aim is to ensure that with the help of the appealing Letterland characters, even the youngest children begin to develop a lasting love of language, love of learning and love of learning to read.

Letterland is a synthetic phonics system. This means that the emphasis is on children learning the actual letter sounds that they will later synthesize into words, and use in due course to crack the code of written English.

Right away Letterland simplifies the learning, introducing a unique visual link to the plain letter shapes by bonding meaningful images into them. The children learn to think of the Letterland characters as normally hidden behind their plain letter shapes, but also there in the imaginary world of Letterland for all to see.

Right away, too, Letterland introduces an economy of learning by providing one simple strategy for discovering and remembering every **a-z** letter sound. Called the 'Sounds Trick', children simply START to say any of the easily learned character names, and then STOP. Immediately, the correct sound is on their lips! Examples: **C**lever **C**at, '**c...**', **P**eter **P**uppy, '**p...**' (both whispered sounds), and **L**ucy **L**amp **L**ight, '**lll...**', **M**unching **M**ike, '**mmm...**', (voiced sounds), etc. So children soon learn all the sounds and, thanks to the paralleled shapes of the Letterland characters, they also readily remember which sound goes with which plain letter shape.

Phonemic awareness and phonics form an essential part of the Early Years Foundation Stage. Letterland teaches children the important 'linking sounds to letters' and 'writing' components within the Communication, Language and Literacy (CLL) area of the Early Years Foundation Stage in a play-based way. In addition, you will find that many features in this handbook also help children to achieve success in other important learning areas, such as Creative Development and Knowledge and Understanding of the World. More on the EYFS on page 12.

Who is Letterland for?

Letterland is well suited to children of all abilities. It is very popular with able children. It can also be life-changing for pre-schoolers with learning difficulties, or from socially and economically disadvantaged backgrounds, or homes where little or no English is spoken, who might otherwise arrive at primary school with poor communicating skills. It can also be very supportive of children with speech and language handicaps as it playfully sets out the building blocks of language and heightens children's attention to them in a wide range of literacy-based activities.

How do you explain to a pre-schooler the dry fact that the plain letter **h** makes a '**hhh**' sound, or why **h** and **H** are both the same letter, *and* ensure that they remember both of these odd facts about those two meaningless abstract letter shapes? How do you make sure your pre-schoolers will even want to know such information? Letterland does all this by turning the letter **h** into a human being who loves to hop along in the Reading Direction in words, and by linking the **h** and **H** shapes through the use of story logic.

The children also 'meet' each character in a scene in the famous *Letterland ABC book*, and seek out objects that begin with the relevant sound. To make sure they also connect each character to its plain letter shape you present it on the reverse side of each card in a set of *Big Picture Code Cards*. (See pages 8-11, and www.letterland.com for it and other accompanying resources.)

Letterland also opens up opportunities for early years practitioners and parents to work in partnership because the language of instruction is storytelling – something easy for teachers, parents and children to all share. So the parents (the children's most enduring educators) can confidently support their child's learning at home – or in the case of Home-schooling parents, implement the whole Letterland programme themselves.

The Letterland Early Years Programme

The materials

Essential

- *Early Years Handbook* (CD audio script available)
- *Letterland ABC Book* or *Phonics Online*
- *Big Picture Code Cards - Lowercase* (**a-z**)
- *Letterland Alphabet Frieze*
- *Handwriting Songs CD* or *Phonics Online*
- *Alphabet Songs CD* or *Phonics Online*

Note: The above materials will be used throughout the *Early Years Handbook* for each Letterland character, so they are not listed under the What you need section on individual letter pages.

Highly recommended

- *Letterland Phonics Online*
- *Early Years Workbooks 1-4*
- *A-Z Copymasters*
- *Early Years Handwriting Copymasters*
- *Alphabet of Rhymes Book*
- *Big Picture Code Cards - Uppercase* (**A-Z**)
- *Action Tricks Poster*
- *First Reading Flashcards*

Notes about the materials

Early Years Handbook

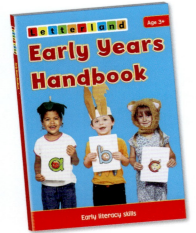

This handbook provides clear guidance on how to introduce all the Letterland **a-z** and **A-Z** characters, including the long vowels (in Letterland 'the Vowel Men'), and includes many practical ideas for follow-up activities and discussion.

One double-page spread is devoted to each Letterland character. The first page contains detailed notes on how to introduce each letter, how to teach the sound it makes in words, and how to write it correctly. The opposite page tells you how to explain the varying capital letter shapes, and is also packed with suggestions for further things to do and to talk about with your class or group to consolidate learning about each letter. To help tie these further activities in with the Early Years

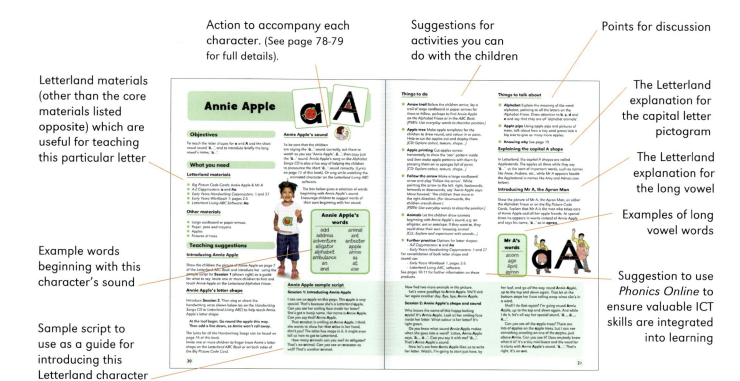

Action to accompany each character. (See page 78-79 for full details).

Suggestions for activities you can do with the children

Points for discussion

Letterland materials (other than the core materials listed opposite) which are useful for teaching this particular letter

The Letterland explanation for the capital letter pictogram

The Letterland explanation for the long vowel

Examples of long vowel words

Example words beginning with this character's sound

Suggestion to use *Phonics Online* **to ensure valuable ICT skills are integrated into learning**

Sample script to use as a guide for introducing this Letterland character

Foundation Stage we have cross-referenced each of the **Things to do** items to one of the EYFS six areas of learning (see page 12). Finally, at the bottom of each spread there is a sample script which is a useful teaching guide during your Letterland sessions. The accompanying CD, read by a native English speaker, is a live example of the style you may like to adopt, and also a model for a way any teacher or parent can get twice as much from this one *Letterland ABC Book*.

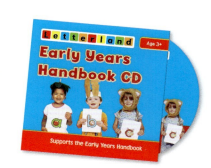

Although the *Early Years Handbook* is laid out in alphabetical order, you may wish to choose a teaching order to complement your own programme. In pre-school settings, focusing on one letter each week generally seems to work well, but be ready to talk about other pictogram characters if asked and to change the pace of learning to fit the children. If some are already familiar with the characters through family or friends, they will still enjoy the repetition and may enjoy helping other children. Being able to write their own name is an important skill in a child's early development. So, when teaching children to write names, associate the Letterland characters with the letters in each child's name. (See also **Long vowels** page 15.)

Letterland ABC Book

The *Letterland ABC book* is an ideal introduction to the alphabet. Throughout this *Early Years Handbook* you will be using illustrations in the *Letterland ABC book* to introduce each new character. You may like to reserve the written text for parents or carers to read aloud and share with children at home. This makes this *Letterland ABC book* a valuable link between home and school.

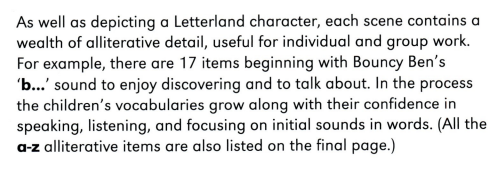

As well as depicting a Letterland character, each scene contains a wealth of alliterative detail, useful for individual and group work. For example, there are 17 items beginning with Bouncy Ben's '**b...**' sound to enjoy discovering and to talk about. In the process the children's vocabularies grow along with their confidence in speaking, listening, and focusing on initial sounds in words. (All the **a-z** alliterative items are also listed on the final page.)

Letterland Phonics Online

This resource to helps you teach and children learn! Enjoy all of the animated stories and songs in one place. Play the phonics games and access the Teacher Toolkit, which is full of supporting resources. (Suitable for whiteboards).

Letterland Alphabet Frieze

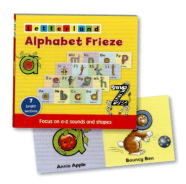

This colourful *Alphabet Frieze* may either be mounted in strips to form a big poster, or in a full **a-z** line. You will find many useful ways to compare and contrast the frieze images with the same characters on the pages of the *ABC Book*.

Handwriting Songs CD

The *Handwriting Songs CD* provides a fun way of learning how to form all 26 letter shapes with the help of the Letterland characters. The words to these songs are on each letter page and are laid out in full on page 76 of this handbook. An animated version is included in *Letterland Phonics Online*.

Alphabet Songs CD

The *Alphabet Songs CD* is intended to help children pronounce all the letter sounds correctly. Each song is sung to the tune of a well-known nursery rhyme. The words for these can be found on page 72. An animated version is included in *Letterland Phonics Online*.

Early Years Workbooks 1-4

These workbooks give children further practice in writing all the letter shapes and help to familiarise them with words beginning with each letter sound. For every letter of the alphabet there are at least two workbook pages. The first one focuses on the letter shape, and the second one on the sound. There are also 31 more open-ended activities which encourage children to think about each letter's sound in other contexts.

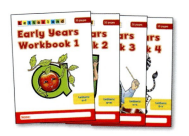

Big Picture Code Cards

There are 46 of these large, easy-to-handle **a-z** cards, including five long vowel cards (the 5 Vowel Men), extra short vowel cards and extra consonants. All the reverse sides show the plain letter shape, so with the flick of your wrist you can make the important transition to plain letter identification. Valuable for finger tracing on both sides and for role play. Useful example words included on each card. The set of 31 *Big Picture Code Cards - Uppercase* are particularly useful for pairing with the lower case cards, finger tracing letter shapes, for revising sounds learnt so far, and for starting children's names.

First Reading Flashcards

These 65 smaller double-sided cards include capital and lower case letters, useful for matching games and many other activities and ideas included in the set, using both the picture and the plain letter sides.

A-Z Copymasters

These 60 copymasters have multiple uses for developing phonemic awareness and fostering observation and comparison skills. The large pictograms with hollow letters are ideal for finger tracing and 'rainbow writing' and there are full instructions and game ideas.

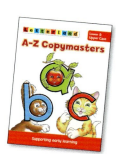

Early Years Handwriting Copymasters

48 photocopiable worksheets of pattern and letter practice for all 26 lowercase letter shapes. Includes a handwriting verse and a pattern practice page for each Letterland character.

Action Tricks Poster

Great visual, auditory, kinesthetic and tactile memory cues for letter shapes and sounds. See page 78 for full details.

Alphabet of Rhymes Book

Alphabet of Rhymes Book is strongly recommended to support your Letterland teaching. It is only referred to in this handbook for certain Letterland characters, but if available, choose any suitable rhyme as part of your **Things to talk about** options.

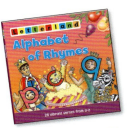

Teaching with Letterland

The 'journey to Letterland'

On your first 'journey to Letterland' with the children, introduce the idea of Letterland by reading them the 'Welcome to Letterland' page of the *Letterland ABC Book*. In subsequent sessions, start with a pretend 'journey to Letterland' routine if time allows. Let children help you to decide how to get there. You may like to mime getting into a bus, train or plane. The children could also close their eyes for a few moments and then open them to arrive in Letterland.

Teaching each alphabet letter

Having 'arrived in Letterland', you are ready to introduce the first Letterlanders. Use the relevant *ABC book* scene and **Session 1** of the sample script provided for each **a-z** letter in this handbook. Follow up with the **Session 2** script and the same *ABC book* scene later on, or on another day, to teach the Letterland character's shape and sound.

The **Things to do** section provides you with ideas for follow-up activities. Each activity is cross-referenced to one of the Early Years Foundation Stage six areas of learning, which are abbreviated as follows:

Personal, Social and Emotional Development (PSE)
Communication, Language and Literacy (CLL)
Mathematical Development (MD)
Knowledge and Understanding of the World (KU)
Physical Development (PD) and **Creative Development** (CD).

For example, the 'Arrow Trail' activity on page 21 relates to the EYFS area of Problem Solving, Reasoning and Numeracy: *Use everyday words to describe position*.

Discussion topics are provided in the **Things to talk about** section, and more general activities are given on page 16 under **Further ideas**.

Letter shapes

Letterland pictograms act as signposts, orientating a child's eyes in the 'Reading Direction'. When teaching letter shapes, remember that the Reading Direction is always from a child's left to right. Take care that you don't accidentally demonstrate a letter stroke in reverse. To avoid this, half turn your back so that you are facing the same way as the children while you make the stroke. Encourage children to finger trace the picture-coded letters on the *Big Picture Code Cards*, *Letterland ABC Book* or the *Letterland Alphabet Frieze*. By following the shape with their finger, children are more likely to form the correct shape when they come to use a pencil. Drawing and painting the characters is also a constructive (and favourite) activity.

The basis of good handwriting is correct pencil grip and correct letter

 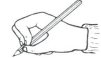

formation. Make sure the children know the correct grip from the start. Once established, a poor grip can all too easily become a life-time habit.

Good relaxed grip   Poor, tense grip

Encourage children to practise the correct grip until they get it right. With children who have not yet established which hand to use, simply place the pencil between both hands and leave the choice to them.

| **Left-handed** | | **Right-handed** | |
| pencil position | page position | pencil position | page position |

If a child forms a letter incorrectly, gently intervene. For example, if he or she mistakenly writes an **e** with a clockwise circle and then breaks the stroke, you could say, 'Eddy Elephant likes you to stroke across his headband *first*, and *end* with his trunk. Let's practise it with one line all the way round.' Also remember that, at this stage, the correct sequence of strokes is more important than neatness.

Use the *A-Z Copymasters, Early Years Workbooks* and *Early Years Handwriting Copymasters* for handwriting practice. Listening to and singing with the *Handwriting Songs CD* or with *Letterland Phonics Online* adds a multi-sensory dimension, reminding children vividly how to form letter shapes correctly.

Letter names and sounds

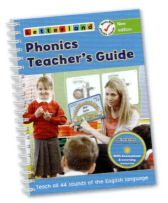

To begin with, it is useful to refer to letters only by their Letterland names, for example, 'Clever Cat' and not 'cee'. Traditional letter names like 'cee', 'aitch', 'em' and 'cue' are initially confusing because they do not match the sounds that letters make in words. In fact, the only useful letter names are the five vowel names since these letter names *do* occur in many common words (e.g. **a**ge, **e**at, **I**, **o**pen and **u**se). These long vowels are introduced briefly in the lesson plans. You could choose to delay teaching them until later, depending on the ages and capabilities of your class. (They will receive fuller focus in the next stage, as set out in the *Letterland Teacher's Guide*.)

Since the 21 consonant *names* ('cee', 'aitch', etc.) are *never* used in reading, it makes sense to delay teaching (or reinforcing) them until children have thoroughly learnt the consonant *sounds*. Before then, these consonant names frequently interfere with the far more important skill of blending letter sounds together to make words, and with reading words with ease.

To avoid any confusion, and to ensure success in learning the all important **a-z** sounds, children can rely on saying the letter's correct sound simply by using the Letterland 'sounds trick' – that is, by just *starting* to say any Letterland character's name.

Action Trick: 'r'

Make a running movement with arms.

A good way to strengthen children's learning of the letter sounds is to teach them the 'Action Tricks' (see page 78) so that they associate each letter with a specific action. The action (e.g. make a running movement with the arms as they say '**rrr**...') helps them them to develop multi-sensory memory cues for the letter sounds.

To ensure that everyone is pronouncing the letter sounds correctly, use the *Alphabet Songs CD* or *Letterland Phonics Online* (see page 10). Song lyrics are on pages 72-75 of this book.

Capital letters

While your focus needs to be on the lowercase letter shapes – because these are the shapes used most in writing – you will want the children to recognise the capital letters and write at least the capital letter that starts a child's name. A helpful guideline for writing any of these capital letter shapes is: 'Always start at the top.' Other capitals the children learn will be interesting for them to know and fun to recognise on signs, etc., but at this stage, learning to write all the capital letters should take lower priority over learning to recognise and write the lowercase letter shapes. The First Reading Flashcards put all these diverse letter shapes (both picture and plain letter sides) in the children's hands and provide many ideas for strengthening their familiarity with both **a-z** and **A-Z**.

Long vowels

The first sounds that children need to know for the five vowels, **a, e, i, o** and **u**, are the short vowel sounds, represented in Letterland by Annie Apple, Eddy Elephant, Impy Ink, Oscar Orange and Uppy Umbrella.

Many words, however, including children's own names, often contain long vowels. By personifying the long vowels as Vowel Men (the only people in Letterland who ever say their *alphabet names* in words), Letterland helps children to understand that each of these five vowel letter shapes actually has two different sounds.

The Vowel Men are namely Mr A (the Apron Man), Mr E (the Easy Magic Man), Mr I (the Ice Cream Man), Mr O (the Old Man) and Mr U (the Uniform Man). By seeing and even dressing up as both long and short vowels, and by comparing them on the *Big Picture Code Cards*, the children will improve their understanding of this dual function of the five vowels.

In this handbook, the Vowel Men are featured on the right hand page of the appropriate spreads. This gives you an opening to talk briefly about each of them, preparing the way for more emphasis on long vowels later (see the *Letterland Teacher's Guide*). However, you may have an **A**mos, S**i**mon, J**o**seph, etc. in your class with long vowels in their names. To Amos you can say, "Your name is special because Mr A himself appears in it instead of Annie Apple" and show him as as stick man on the vowel.

Amos
Simon
Joseph
Eve
Eugene

Parental involvement

Encourage parents and carers to read with their children from a wide range of materials, including books, newspapers, catalogues, magazines and packaging. Literacy skills are the foundation of a child's future attainment, so it is a great help to children when home and school join together to support their reading, writing and spelling. Page 80 sets out some guidelines for parents and carers. You may like to photocopy this page and give it to the parents, or use it as a starting point to write your own information sheet for them.

Your own ideas

This handbook is just intended to help you get started. You will soon develop your own style and a range of additional activities. For example, you may choose to teach the letters at a different pace, covering more than one letter a week, or to go more slowly. It's up to you to decide!

Further ideas

As soon as the children have 'met' several of the Letterland characters, opportunities arise to introduce the characters into general activities. The possibilities are endless, but here are a number of suggestions.

Display area

Collect pictures and objects beginning with the letter currently being taught. Ask children to bring in items for 'Show and Tell' that start with the focus sound. Where time allows, make a really big collage or painting of the pictogram character. It will provide an eye-catching focus on the initial sound which is common to all the pictures and objects displayed around it.

Tiny object collection

Make a row of the letters learned so far using the *Big Picture Code Cards*. Ask children to place small items beginning with that letter sound under each card e.g. arrow, button, conker, (tiny toy) dog, egg-shell, etc. (Where objects are difficult to find, you can draw them or use pictures.) Remove the objects and assign specific children to re-allocate them. This activity can provide a useful form of revision of both letter sounds and the alphabet sequence.

Dressing up

Add steadily to a 'Clever Cat's Costume Box' by collecting items such as a toy firefighter's helmet and making animal ears, masks, etc. Each new prop will add to the possibilities of Letterland-related activities in free play. Parents and carers usually enjoy being enlisted to sew or create these props.

Miming without props

Once the children are familiar with a few of the Letterland characters, ask one or more children to mime how the letter of their choice behaves. The other children then have to guess who they are. Alternatively, children can do the 'Action Tricks' (see page 78). The rest of the group must say the sound. Repeat this activity as children become familiar with more letters.

Painting a–z

Pencil in the letters, big and bold, as guidelines for children's paintings. Children can go over them in paint and add the pictogram details. You could keep their letter paintings and use them later on to build three-letter words.

Photographic a–z

Take photographs of the children pretending to be all the different Letterland characters. They could be holding or wearing *Big Picture Code Cards* and/or wearing appropriate items from 'Clever Cat's Costume Box' (see **Dressing up** on page 17). Put all the photos into an album in alphabetical order for use as a unique class ABC. This can then be used with your current class, and for future ones, helping to inspire incoming children. You could also take photos of children doing the **a-z** Action Tricks. See page 78 for details.

Storytelling

Start a story which takes place in Letterland. For example, 'One day after work, Firefighter Fred decided to go fishing. On his way to the river he met...?' Children then supply the next words. Help them, if necessary, using alliterative words (see the example words on the relevant letter page) or with whatever other ideas come to mind. Their contributions need not include words beginning with a particular sound. The aim here is to help them to develop story-telling techniques, and to contribute parts to a whole story.

Stories by older children

Enlist children from a local primary school to write and illustrate original stories – in prose or verse – featuring Letterland characters for your Early Years class. This can have very positive benefits for all concerned. Your children will love sharing Letterland with older children. The older children, in turn, will be motivated to write clearly, add appropriate illustrations and present their stories attractively for their special new readership.

Letter spotting

The first time children recognise a letter in their environment, it is like seeing a friendly face in a crowd! Provide lots of opportunities for children to study the various signs and notices that surround them – in the classroom and out in the shops – and encourage them to do some 'letter spotting'.

Fund-raising

Parents can run Letterland stalls at fund-raising events, for example, a 'Clever Cat's Crafts Stall' or a 'Harry Hat Man's Hot Dog Stall'. They may even enjoy impersonating Letterland characters, thereby helping to make any fund-raising event a bit different!

Reading labels

By labelling items around the room, you convey the fact that spoken words can also be written. Encourage children to read labels, even if at this stage they can only 'read' them by knowing their place on the wall and recognising the first letter.

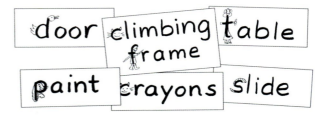

Knowing why

Each day, to make sure the children realise the relevance of their activities to the letter they have been learning about, talk about all the things they have been doing. For instance, ask, 'Why did we play that 'Leaping up' game and paint a lighthouse and write letters and make little lambs and put labels on things? Yes, because all those things start with Lucy Lamp Light's sound!'

Assessment

Letterland Phonics Online has built-in assessment on **a-z** letter sounds, shapes, long and short vowel sounds and first word-building skills. You may also like to use the *First Reading Flashcards* or the *Magnetic Letters* to assess how well the children have learnt their letters so far, creating a game-like atmosphere as you do so.

Annie Apple

Objectives

To teach the letter shapes for **a** and **A** and the short vowel sound '**ă**...', and to introduce briefly the long vowel's name, '**ā**...'.

What you need

Letterland materials

- *Big Picture Code Cards:* Annie Apple & Mr A
- *A-Z Copymasters:* **a** and **Aa**
- *Early Years Handwriting Copymasters:* 1 and 27
- *Early Years Workbook 1:* pages 2-5
- *Letterland Phonics Online:* **Aa**

Other materials

- Large cardboard or paper arrows
- Paper, pens and crayons
- Apples
- Pictures of trees

Teaching suggestions

Introducing Annie Apple

Show the children the picture of Annie Apple on page 7 of the *Letterland ABC Book* and introduce her using the sample script for **Session 1** (shown right) as a guide for what to say. Invite one or more children to find and touch Annie Apple on the *Letterland Alphabet Frieze*.

Annie Apple's letter shape

Introduce **Session 2**. Then sing or chant the handwriting verse shown below (as on the *Handwriting Songs CD* or *Letterland Phonics Online*) to help teach Annie Apple's letter shape:

**At the leaf begin. Go round the apple this way.
Then add a line down, so Annie won't roll away.**

The lyrics for all the Handwriting Songs can be found on page 76 of this book.
Invite one or more children to finger trace Annie's letter shape on the *Letterland ABC Book* or on both sides of the *Big Picture Code Card*.

Annie Apple's sound

To be sure that the children are saying the '**ă**...' sound correctly, ask them to watch as you say 'Annie Apple', **ă**...', then copy just the '**ă**...' sound. Annie Apple's song on the *Alphabet Songs CD* is also a fun way of helping the children to pronounce the short '**ă**...' sound correctly. (Lyrics on page 72 of this book). Or sing while watching the animated character on *Phonics Online*.

The box below gives a selection of words beginning with Annie Apple's sound. Encourage children to suggest words of their own beginning with her sound.

Annie Apple's words

add	animal
address	ant
adventure	anteater
alligator	apple
alphabet	arrow
ambulance	as
an	at
and	axe

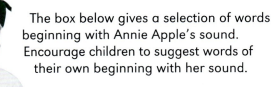

Annie Apple sample script

Session 1: Introducing Annie Apple

I can see an **a**pple on this page. This **a**pple is *very* special. That's because she's a *Letterland* **a**pple. Can you see her smiling face *inside* her letter? She's got a *lovely* name. Her name is **A**nnie **A**pple. Can you say that? **A**nnie **A**pple.

That **a**crobat is smiling at **A**nnie **A**pple. I think she wants to show her that **a**tlas in her hand, don't you? The atlas has maps in it. It might even tell us how to get to Letterland.

How many **a**nimals can you see? An **a**lligator? That's an **a**nimal. Can you see an **a**nteater as well? That's another **a**nimal.

Things to do

- **Arrow trail** Before the children arrive, lay a trail of large cardboard or paper arrows for them to follow, perhaps to find Annie Apple on the *Alphabet Frieze* or in the *ABC Book*.
  [*PSRN: Use everyday words to describe position.*]

- **Apple tree** Make apple templates for the children to draw round, and colour in or paint. Help to cut the apples out and display them.
  [*CD: Explore colour, texture, shape...*]

- **Apple printing** Cut apples across horizontally to show the 'star' pattern inside and then make apple patterns with them by pressing them on to sponges full of paint.
  [*CD: Explore colour, texture, shape...*]

- **Follow the arrow** Make a large cardboard arrow and play 'Follow the arrow'. While pointing the arrow to the left, right, backwards, forwards or downwards, say 'Annie Apple says: Move forward.' The children then move in the right direction. (For downwards, the children crouch down.)
  [*PSRN: Use everyday words to describe position.*]

- **Animals** Let the children draw animals beginning with Annie Apple's sound, e.g. an alligator, ant or antelope. If they want to, they could draw their own 'amazing animal'.
  [*CLL: Explore and experiment with sounds...*]

- **Further practice** Options for letter shapes:
  – *A-Z Copymasters:* **a** and **Aa**
  – *Early Years Handwriting Copymasters:* 1 and 27
  For consolidation of both letter shape and sound use:
  – *Early Years Workbook 1*, pages 2-5.
  – *Letterland Phonics Online*.
  See pages 10-11 for further information on these products.

Things to talk about

- **Alphabet** Explain the meaning of the word alphabet, pointing to all the letters on the *Alphabet Frieze*. Draw attention to **b**, **c**, **d** and **e** and say that they are all 'alphabet animals'.

- **Apple pips** Using apple pips and pictures of trees, talk about how a tiny seed grows into a big tree to give us many more apples.

- **Knowing why** See page 19.

Explaining the capital A shape

In Letterland, the capital A shapes are called Applestands. The apples sit there while they say 'ă...' at the start of important words, such as names like Anne, Andrew, etc., while Mr A appears beside the Applestand in names like Amy and Adrian (see below).

Introducing Mr A, the Apron Man

Show the picture of Mr A, the Apron Man, on either the Alphabet Frieze or on the Big Picture Code Cards. Explain that Mr A is the man who takes care of Annie Apple and all her apple friends. At special times he appears in words instead of Annie Apple and says his name, 'ā...' as in **apron**.

Mr A's words
acorn
age
April
apron

Now find two more animals in the picture.
Let's wave goodbye to **A**nnie **A**pple. We'll visit her again another day. Bye, bye, **A**nnie **A**pple.

Session 2: Annie Apple's shape and sound

Who knows the name of this happy-looking **a**pple? It's **A**nnie **A**pple. Look at her smiling face inside her letter. What colour is her letter? It's light green.

Do you know what sound **A**nnie **A**pple makes when she goes into a word? Listen, **A**nnie **A**pple says, 'ă..., ă...'. Can you say it with me? 'ă...'. That's **A**nnie **A**pple's sound.

Now let's see how **A**nnie **A**pple likes us to write her letter. Watch, I'm going to start just here, by

her leaf, and go *all* the way round **A**nnie **A**pple, *up* to the top and *down* again. That bit at the bottom stops her from rolling away when she's in a word.

Shall I do that again? I'm going round **A**nnie **A**pple, *up* to the top and *down* again. And while I do it, let's all say her special sound, 'ă..., ă..., ă...'.

Can you see all the **a**pple trees? There are lots of **a**pples on the **a**pple trees, but I can see something crawling on one of the **a**pples, just above Annie. Can you see it? Does anybody know what it is? It's a tiny mini-beast and the word for it starts with **A**nnie **A**pple's sound, 'ă...'. That's right. It's an **a**nt.

Bouncy Ben

Objective

To teach the letter shapes and sound for **b** and **B**.

What you need

Letterland materials

- *Big Picture Code Cards:* Bouncy Ben
- *A-Z Copymasters:* **b** and **Bb**
- *Early Years Handwriting Copymasters:* 2 and 28
- *Early Years Workbook 1:* pages 6-7
- *Letterland Phonics Online:* **Bb**

Other materials

- Washing-up liquid
- Blue paint in a large jar
- Straws
- Ingredients for making biscuits or buns
- Bread, butter and blackberry jam
- Blue balloon

Teaching suggestions

Introducing Bouncy Ben

Show the children the picture of Bouncy Ben on page 9 of the *Letterland ABC Book* and introduce him using the sample script for **Session 1** (shown right) as a guide for what to say. Invite one or more children to find and touch Bouncy Ben's face on the *Letterland Alphabet Frieze*.

Bouncy Ben's letter shape

Introduce **Session 2**. Then sing or chant the handwriting verse shown below (as on the *Handwriting Songs CD* or *Letterland Phonics Online*) to help teach Bouncy Ben's letter shape:

> **Brush down Ben's big, long ears.**
> **Go up and round his head so his face appears!**

Invite one or more children to finger trace Ben's letter shape on the *Letterland ABC Book* or on both sides of the *Big Picture Code Card*.

Bouncy Ben's sound

To say Bouncy Ben's sound correctly, tell the children to keep their faces still, with their mouths almost completely closed to keep any tendency to add 'uh' to a minimum. In reading, too much 'uh' sound will make blending difficult, e.g. 'buh-e-d' instead of 'be...d'. Use the Bouncy Ben song on the *Alphabet Songs CD* or *Letterland Phonics Online* to help the children achieve the correct sound.

Bouncy Ben's words

baby	blue
bad	boat
balance	bounce
ball	bread
bat	breakfast
beautiful	bridge
bed	brown
bee	bubble
big	bun
bird	bus
birthday	butter
biscuit	butterfly

Bouncy Ben sample script

Session 1: Introducing Bouncy Ben

I can see a **b**lue letter on this page. And I can see somebody looking out of the letter. Can you see two **b**lue eyes looking out of the letter? Yes, those **b**lue eyes **b**elong to a Letterland rabbit called **B**ouncy **B**en.

Can you see his **b**lue **b**all at the **b**ottom of the page? He **b**ounced that **b**all into the **b**ushes. Shall we put *our* hand out and pretend *we've* got a **b**all and **b**ounce it?

Bounce, **b**ounce, **b**ounce goes the **b**all. That's right. Put your **b**all away now, and give your hand a rest.

Bouncy **B**en loves playing with a **b**all. He does

Things to do

● **Bouncing** Suggest that all the children bounce like Bouncy Ben with both feet together, while making 'b...' sounds. Then let them try bouncing backwards: much harder!
Warn them not to bump into each other!
[PD: Move with control and coordination.]

● **Building bridges** Provide construction toys such as building blocks and ask the children to build bridges with them.
[KU: Build and construct with a wide range of objects...]

● **Butterfly pictures** Help the children to make 'butterfly pictures'. Fold a sheet of paper in half, then unfold it. Add a blob of paint on one half. Fold the paper along the crease, smooth down and open again. Add another colour, fold and smooth down again. Open up the paper and add eyes and feelers. You may need to help with the finishing touches!
[PSRN: Talk about, recognise and recreate simple patterns.]

● **Bubble pictures** Mix washing-up liquid and blue paint in a large jar. The children pretend to be Bouncy Ben while they blow into the paint with a straw until bubbles overflow. (First check that the children know the difference between blowing and sucking!) Press a sheet of paper onto the paint bubbles over the top of the jar and then remove it.
[CD: Explore colour, shape, form...]

● **Cookery** Help the children to make b-shaped biscuits or buns. They could also eat bread, butter and blackberry jam.
[KU: Investigate objects and materials ...]

● **Further practice** Options for letter shapes:
 – *A-Z Copymasters:* **b** and **Bb**
 – *Early Years Handwriting Copymasters:* 2 and 28
For consolidation of both letter shape and sound use:
 – *Early Years Workbook 1*, pages 6-7.
 – *Letterland Phonics Online.*

Things to talk about

● **Breakfast** Talk about what the children like to eat for breakfast. What do they think Bouncy Ben would have for breakfast? For instance, you could ask, 'Would he have bread/bacon/ baked beans/?' ('Yes.') or 'Would he have cornflakes/eggs/ sausages?' ('No.')

● **Balloons** Blow up a big blue balloon and talk about it getting bigger. This can lead on to looking for other words beginning with Bouncy Ben's sound.

● **Knowing why** See page 19.

Explaining the capital B shape

Bouncy Ben's head is still in the same position in his capital letter shape. The only difference now is that he is balancing his 'best blue ball' between his 'big brown ears'. Explain that Bouncy Ben does this whenever he starts an important word such as a name. Let the children take turns at being Bouncy Ben by balancing a ball or balloon on their heads between upraised arms, as in the capital **B**.

---

something special with his **b**ig **b**lue **b**all as well. Sometimes he **b**alances his **b**lue **b**all on top of his head.

Session 2: Bouncy Ben's shape and sound

Let's have a look at **B**ouncy **B**en's **b**lue letter on this page again. Shall we draw it?

I'm going to start at the top of **B**ouncy **B**en's **b**ig **b**rown ear, go *down* his ear, and then I'm going to go **b**ack up *over* his face... and I stop just under his chin.

And while I do it this time, I'm going to say **B**ouncy **B**en's special sound. You listen. **B**ouncy **B**en says 'b..., b..., b...'. It's a very *short* little sound. Can you say his short little sound with me? 'B..., b..., b...'. Yes, **B**ouncy **B**en says, 'b...'.

I can see something red and yellow right at the top of the page. It uses its red and yellow wings to fly. Do you know what it's called? That's right. It's a **b**utterfly, a **b**eautiful **b**utterfly.

Wait a minute. That word **butterfly** starts with Bouncy **B**en's sound, doesn't it! 'B..., b...' **b**utterfly. That's the sound **B**en always makes in words!

And can you see something else that flies in the sky? It has a sting. What's it called? A **b**ee! That's right. It's a **b**uzzy **b**ee.

Who can remember how we draw **B**ouncy **B**en again? Where do we start? Right at the tip of his **b**ig long ears. We go *right* down his ear, then up *around* his face so he is ready to say 'b..., b..., b...' for **B**ouncy **B**en.

Clever Cat

Objective

To teach the letter shapes and sound for **c** and **C**.

What you need

Letterland materials

- *Big Picture Code Cards:* Clever Cat
- *A-Z Copymasters:* **c** and **Cc**
- *Early Years Handwriting Copymasters:* 3 & 29
- *Early Years Workbook 1:* pages 8-9
- *Alphabet of Rhymes Book*
- *Letterland Phonics Online:* **Cc**

Other materials

- Pictures of cats
- Paper plates
- Elastic or tape
- Modelling dough
- Coloured pens or crayons
- Comics
- Biscuits or cup cakes
- Icing sugar and small sweets

Teaching suggestions

Introducing Clever Cat

Show the children the picture of Clever Cat on page 11 of the *Letterland ABC Book* and introduce her using the sample script for **Session 1** (shown right) as a guide. Invite one or more children to find and touch Clever Cat on the *Alphabet Frieze*.

Clever Cat's letter shape

Introduce **Session 2**. Then sing or chant the handwriting verse shown below (as on the *Handwriting Songs CD* or *Letterland Phonics Online*) to help teach Clever Cat's letter shape:

Curve round Clever Cat's face to begin.
Then gently tickle her under her chin.

Invite one or more children to finger trace Clever Cat's letter shape on the *Letterland ABC Book* or on both sides of the *Big Picture Code Card*.

Clever Cat's sound

Clever Cat's sound is an *unvoiced* sound. Make sure that the children practise it in a whisper. It is very important, when it comes to blending sounds, that no child says 'cuh'. Take care especially when singing Clever Cat's song from the *Alphabet Songs CD* or *Letterland Phonics Online*. Stop singing to *whisper* the 'c...' sound.

Clever Cat's words

cake	clock
can	clothes
candles	cold
cap	colour
car	come
castle	cook
cat	count
clean	cross
clever	cuddle
climb	cup

Clever Cat sample script

Session 1: Introducing Clever Cat

Let's look at this page. Can you see that **c**at? Have you got a **c**at? Isn't this **c**at a *lovely* **c**at! She has a red letter on her head. That's because she's a *Letterland* **c**at.

Look, she has just settled down to have a **c**up of **c**ocoa outside the Letterland **c**astle. What else has she brought with her? She has a **c**ucumber sandwich, a yummy **c**ream **c**ake and her **c**rossword puzzle.

She even remembered to bring along her favourite **c**ushion. **C**lever **C**at thinks of everything. That's why people call her **C**lever **C**at.

Can you see some white things in the sky? What are they? That's right. They're **c**louds in the sky. Sometimes there are lots of dark **c**louds in

Things to do

- **Cat collages** Make cat collages by asking the children to draw cats or use cat pictures cut out from cards, calendars and magazines. Mount and display them.
  [CD: Explore colour, texture, shape...]

- **Paper plate face** Help the children to draw and colour in Clever Cat's face on the back of a paper plate. Then add ears, whiskers, etc., using scraps of paper or fur fabric and string. They can be made into masks by cutting holes for the eyes and adding elastic or tape ties.
  [CD: Explore colour, texture, shape...]

- **Cut-outs** Let the children use modelling dough to cut out cat shapes or to make pretend cakes.
  [PD: Handle tools, objects, construction...]

- **Cookery** The children can make Clever Cat's face on plain biscuits or on cup cakes using icing and small sweets.
  [KU: Look closely at similarities, differences...]

- **Comics** Look at some comics and decide which one Clever Cat might like best.
  [CD: Explore colour, texture, shape...]

- **Further practice** Options for letter shapes:
  – *A-Z Copymasters:* **c** and **Cc**
  – *Early Years Handwriting Copymasters:* 3 and 29.
  For consolidation of both letter shape and sound use:
  – *Early Years Workbook 1*, pages 8-9.
  – *Letterland Phonics Online.*

Things to talk about

- **Clever Cat's sound** Talk about what sound cats usually make and then explain that Clever Cat never miaows, but says 'c..., c...' instead. She is the only cat that does this.

- **Cats** Find out if any of the children have a cat at home. Talk about the things that cats like to eat and drink, such as fish, milk or cream. Explain that because she is a Letterland cat, Clever Cat only eats food that begins with her sound, and help the children to think what she would like, e.g. **cream cakes**, **crisps**, **carrots**, **cucumbers**, **cauliflower**, etc.

- **Caterpillars** Bring in some caterpillars (and leaves) in a suitable clear container. Talk about their colours and movements and explain how they turn into butterflies or moths.

- **Rhyme** If available, read the Clever Cat poem from the *Alphabet of Rhymes* Book to the children. See page 11.

- **Knowing why** See page 19.

Explaining the capital C shape

Explain to the children that whenever Clever Cat starts important words such as names, she takes a deep breath and gets bigger.

---

the sky. What **c**omes out of the **c**louds? Yes. The rain **c**omes. Will it rain today? No, the sky is blue.

Look at the picture. Do you like **C**lever **C**at's **c**ar? It's nice and **c**olourful, isn't it? Now, let's wave goodbye. Goodbye, **C**lever **C**at.

Session 2: Clever Cat's shape and sound

Can anyone tell us the name of the lovely **c**at here in this picture? Yes, **C**lever **C**at. What's she doing here? Yes, she's having a **c**up of **c**ocoa. Where does **C**lever **C**at live? In Letterland!

Clever **C**at is a very *special* **c**at because she is a *Letterland* **c**at. I've got a **c**at and my **c**at says 'Miaow'. But this **c**at is far too **c**lever to say 'Miaow'. **C**lever **C**at is *so* **c**lever that she makes a special sound instead, like this, '**c**..., **c**..., **c**...'. Can you make that sound with me? Just whisper it, '**c**..., **c**..., **c**...'. That's right. Can you hear her

little '**c**...' sound two times as you say her name? Listen, **C**...lever **C**...at?

Let's stroke her, shall we? She likes us to stroke her in a very special way, around her letter. We start by her ear, we go *over* to the other ear, go *round* her face, and we stop under her chin. That's it. Shall we do it again? Let's make her special sound, '**c**..., **c**..., **c**...' as we go round.

Let's see what else we can find in our picture that begins with **C**lever **C**at's sound.

What are those white things up in the sky? **C**louds, yes!

And what is **C**lever **C**at going to eat on that table? **C**ream **c**akes! Most **c**ats we know would never eat **c**ream **c**akes. But **C**lever **C**at does. Why? Because she's a *Letterland* **c**at. So she likes to eat anything that begins with her sound. **C**ream **c**akes and **c**ucumber sandwiches for our **C**lever **C**at.

Dippy Duck

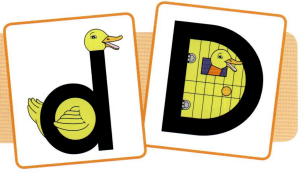

Objective

To teach the letter shapes and sound for **d** and **D**.

What you need

Letterland materials

- *Big Picture Code Cards:* Dippy Duck
- *A-Z Copymasters:* **d** and **Dd**
- *Early Years Handwriting Copymasters:* 4 and 30
- *Early Years Workbook 1:* pages 10-11
- *Alphabet of Rhymes Book*
- *Letterland Phonics Online:* **Dd**

Other materials

- Egg boxes or yellow tissue paper
- Yellow felt or buttons
- Modelling dough
- Duck-shaped cutters (if available)
- 6 shoe boxes
- Dice
- Pictures of ducks
- Paper 'dinner' plates and dishes

Teaching suggestions

Introducing Dippy Duck

Show the children the picture of Dippy Duck on page 13 of the *Letterland ABC Book* and introduce her using the sample script for **Session 1** (shown right) as a guide for what to say. Invite one or more children to find and touch Dippy Duck and her Duck Door on the *Letterland Alphabet Frieze*.

Dippy Duck's letter shape

Introduce **Session 2**. Then sing or chant the handwriting verse shown below (on the *Handwriting Songs CD* or *Letterland Phonics Online*) to help teach Dippy Duck's letter shape:

Draw Dippy Duck's back. Go round her tum.
Go up to her head. Then down you come!

Invite one or more children to finger trace Dippy Duck's letter shape on the *Letterland ABC Book* or on both sides of the *Big Picture Code Cards*. Learning the difference between **b** and **d** takes time. The key to correct **d**-shapes is the starting point (Dippy Duck's back) and the discovery that Dippy Duck can be found in a child's right (writing) hand. To see her letter, children just lift their index finger briefly. Left-handers simply copy their free hand!

Dippy Duck's sound

It is very difficult to avoid adding an unwanted 'uh' sound when making Dippy Duck's letter sound. Try to ensure that the children say 'd...' through closed teeth. This way they will manage to keep the 'uh' to a minimum. Dippy Duck's song on the *Alphabet Songs CD* or *Letterland Phonics Online* provides useful practice in her 'd...' sound.

Dippy Duck's words

Daddy	dish	down
daffodil	doctor	draw
daisy	dog	dress
dance	doll	drink
day	donkey	drum
dinner	door	duck

Dippy Duck sample script

Session 1: Introducing Dippy Duck

Let's look at this page. What can we see? Yes, there's a yellow **d**uck on this page. Have *you* ever seen a **d**uck swimming on the water?

Look at the **d**uck's feet: they are webbed feet. Webbed feet help **d**ucks to swim and **d**ive **d**own in the water. **D**ucks **d**ip their beaks into the water to **d**rink.

This is our Letterland **d**uck. Her name is **D**ippy **D**uck. She's called **D**ippy **D**uck because she **d**ips her beak into the water to **d**rink and to search for food in the **d**uck pond.

Things to do

- **Duck heads** Make paper duck heads for the children to wear on their right index fingers. Hold them in place with sticky tape.

- **Dippy Duck dance** Let the children waddle about like Dippy Duck, making 'd...' sounds at the same time.
  [PD: Move with control and coordination.]

- **Daffodil or daisy pictures** The children cut out petal shapes to make a flower. For a daffodil, you can use part of an egg box painted yellow for the trumpet, or use tissue paper. Use a circle of yellow felt or a button for the daisy's centre.
  [PD: Move with control and coordination.]

- **Dough ducks** Let the children use modelling dough to make dough ducks. Use duck-shaped cutters, if available.
  [PD: Handle tools, objects, construction...]

- **Dice game** Remove the lids of six shoe boxes and number them one to six. Line them up on the floor. The children can take turns to throw a die and then try to throw a ball into the box marked with the same number.
  [PSRN: Recognise numerals 1 to 9.]

- **Duck den** Turn a corner of the room into a duck den for the week. Add pictures of ducks on the wall, and put out dinner plates and dishes for serving 'Dippy Duck's dinner'.
  [CLL: Explore and experiment with sounds...]

- **Further practice** Options for letter shapes:
  - *A-Z Copymasters:* **d** and **Dd**, **b** and **d**.
  - *Early Years Handwriting Copymasters:* 4 and 30

For consolidation of both letter shape and sound use:
  - *Early Years Workbook 1*, pages 10-11.
  - *Letterland Phonics Online.*

Things to talk about

- **Ducks** Talk about ducks and how they hatch from eggs like chickens. Tell the children that little ducklings are covered with down (very soft, fluffy feathers) and know how to swim right away.

- **Rhyme** If available, read the Dippy Duck poem from the *Alphabet of Rhymes* Book to the children and then try learning the lines together.

- **Dippy Duck's words** Help the children to think of words beginning with Dippy Duck's sound. Give hints using the box on page 26.

- **Ugly Duckling** Tell the story of 'The Ugly Duckling'.

- **Ducks' song** Teach the song 'Five little ducks went swimming one day'.

- **Knowing why** Reminder: see page 19.

Explaining the capital D shape

To help the children to remember the capital D shape, tell them that the funny-shaped door with Dippy Duck's head poking out is Dippy Duck's duck door. When they see it at the beginning of a word, they should think of Dippy Duck saying '**d**...' just inside her door.

Dippy **D**uck can **d**ive in the **d**uck pond too. Let's say our Letterland **d**uck's name again. Her name is **D**ippy **D**uck.

Session 2: Dippy Duck's shape and sound

Who can remember the name of our **d**uck? Yes, it's **D**ippy **D**uck.

Dippy **D**uck is a special **d**uck because she *never* quacks. She makes a very quiet sound, listen. **D**ippy **D**uck says '**d**..., **d**..., **d**...'.

She says '**d**...' when she is **d**iving. She says '**d**...' when she **d**ips her beak into her **d**uck pond to search for food.

Can you say her '**d**...' sound with me while I **d**raw round her letter? I'll start to **d**raw *over* **D**ippy **D**uck's back, I'll go *under* her body, *up* to her head and I then stroke her feathers *down*. **D**id you say '**d**...' while I **d**rew **D**ippy **D**uck's letter?

Let's **d**o it again. Start to **d**raw *over* **D**ippy **D**uck's back, *under* her body, *up* to her head and then stroke her feathers *down* again.

Look, can you see the **d**oor on her house? It's **D**ippy **D**uck's **d**oor. When she goes in there, there's a **d**elicious **d**inner of **d**uckweed and **d**andelions waiting for **D**ippy **D**uck.

Eddy Elephant

Objectives

To teach the letter shapes for **e** and **E** and the short vowel sound 'ĕ...', and to introduce briefly the long vowel's name, 'ē...'.

What you need

Letterland materials

- *Big Picture Code Cards*: Eddy Elephant & Mr E
- *A-Z Copymasters*: **e** and **Ee**
- *Early Years Handwriting Copymasters:* 5 and 31
- *Early Years Workbook 1*: pages 12-13
- *Letterland Phonics Online*: **Ee**

Other materials

- Large egg-shaped pieces of paper or card
- 3 egg boxes
- 12 balls: 6 each of 2 colours
- Egg shells
- Cotton wool
- Cress seed

Teaching suggestions

Introducing Eddy Elephant

Show the children the picture of Eddy Elephant on page 15 of the *Letterland ABC Book* and introduce him using the sample script for **Session 1** (shown right) as a guide for what to say. Invite one or more children to find and touch Eddy Elephant's face and trunk on the *Alphabet Frieze*.

Eddy Elephant's letter shape

Introduce **Session 2**. Then sing or chant the handwriting verse shown below (on the *Handwriting Songs CD* or *Letterland Phonics Online)* to help teach Eddy Elephant's letter shape:

Ed has a headband. Draw it and then stroke round his head and his trunk to the end.

Invite one or more children to finger trace Eddy Elephant's letter shape on the *Letterland ABC Book* or on both sides of the *Big Picture Code Card*.

Eddy Elephant's sound

Tell the children that if they ever forget Eddy Elephant's sound, they just need to *start* saying his name and the right sound will come out of their mouths.

Eddy's song on the *Alphabet Songs CD* or *Letterland Phonics Online* will also help the child to achieve the correct sound.

Eddy Elephant's words

egg	engine
elbow	enjoy
elephant	enter
eleven	envelope
empty	every
end	exit

Eddy Elephant sample script

Session 1: Introducing Eddy Elephant

You will like this **e**lephant. Do you know what his name is? It's **E**ddy **E**lephant. He is doing something very difficult in this picture. He's using his trunk to throw and catch four big Easter **e**ggs. Let's count them. One, two, three, four.

Do you think **E**ddy can catch all the **e**ggs before they drop to the ground and break? **E**veryone is looking at **E**ddy **E**lephant to see if he can do it. I couldn't do it. Could you?

The Easter **e**ggs have lovely patterns on them. One has spots, another has stars, one is stripy and one has flowers. Which pattern do you like best? If you look carefully, you will find some more **e**ggs in the picture, snuggled in a nest. How many can you count?

Things to do

- **Egg patterns** Provide the children with egg-shaped pieces of paper or card for them to decorate with patterns. Start a pattern at the top for them and ask them to try to make more rows that look the same.
  [CLL: Use a pencil and hold it effectively...]

- **Egg box game** To play the egg box maths game, you need three empty egg boxes, six balls of one colour and six more of another. (If necessary, you can make these with screwed-up pieces of paper.) Get the children to see how many different ways they can fill the boxes, such as 2 red + 4 blue, or 3 red + 3 blue.
  [PSRN: Begin to relate addition to combining two groups of objects...]

- **Egg heads** Help the children to make 'egg heads'. Fill clean, empty egg shells with cotton wool. Using a felt pen, let the children *gently* draw faces on the shells and place them in egg cups. Dampen the cotton wool for them to sprinkle on cress seed and leave to let the 'hair' grow.
  [KU: Find out about and identify some features of living things...]

- **Further practice** Options for letter shapes:
  – *A-Z Copymasters:* **e** and **Ee**
  – *Early Years Handwriting Copymasters:* 5 and 31
  For consolidation of both letter shape and sound use:
  – *Early Years Workbook 1*, pages 12-13.
  – *Letterland Phonics Online*.

Things to talk about

- **Elephants** Talk about elephants and ask if anyone has seen one at the zoo. Ask if they know why elephants need a long bendy trunk.

- **Action rhyme** Teach the children the action rhyme 'An elephant goes likes this and that'.

- **Eddy's objects** Help the children to think of objects beginning with Eddy's letter.

Explaining the capital E shape

Eddy Elephant is very proud of his 'elephant on end' trick. He sits down and points everything – his trunk and all his feet – in the Reading Direction whenever he starts an important word.

Introducing Mr E, the Easy Magic Man

Show the children the picture of Mr E, the Easy Magic Man, on either the *Letterland Alphabet Frieze* or on the *Big Picture Code Cards*. Explain that Mr E looks after Eddy Elephant and has taught him his 'elephant on end' trick. At special times Mr E appears instead of Eddy Elephant and says his name, 'ē ...' as in **easy**.

Mr E's words

Easter
easy
eat
even

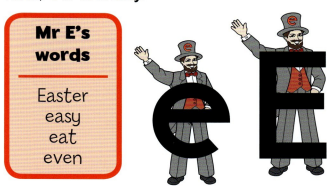

Do you know what colour they are?

Who else can you see that we have already met? Can you see Bouncy Ben on his bike? And Clever Cat coming to take a closer look at **E**ddy **E**lephant? Look, Dippy Duck is flying down into the fairground as well. And there are lots more Letterland people and animals in the picture. We will be meeting them later on in this book. Let's say goodbye now to **E**ddy **E**lephant. Good bye, **E**ddy **E**lephant.

Session 2: Eddy Elephant's shape and sound

Let's have another look at **E**ddy **E**lephant. Shall we make his red letter? Start by his ear, go *across* his forehead, go *over* the top of his head and around, and stop at his mouth just underneath his trunk. Shall we do it again? Start by his ear.

Go *across* his forehead first..., and then *over* the top of his head and round, and stop by his mouth. That's **E**ddy **E**lephant.

Shall I tell you a secret about Letterland animals and people? Did you know, you can always find out what sound they make in words by just *starting* to say their names? Let's just start to say '**E**ddy **E**lephant' and see what sound we make. Be ready to put your hand over your mouth so only the first sound comes out. Ready... 'Ĕ ...'! Yes, **E**ddy **E**lephant's sound is 'ĕ ..., ĕ ..., ĕ .... Shall we say it while I stroke his letter, ĕ ..., ĕ ..., ĕ ...'.

No wonder **E**ddy **E**lephant likes playing with **e**ggs. Can you think why he's playing with **e**ggs? It's because the word **eggs** starts with **E**ddy **E**lephant's sound. So of course **E**ddy **E**lephant **e**njoys playing with **e**ggs!

Firefighter Fred

Objective

To teach the letter shapes and sound for **f** and **F**.

What you need

Letterland materials

- *Big Picture Code Cards*: Firefighter Fred
- *A-Z Copymasters*: **f** and **Ff**
- *Early Years Handwriting Copymasters:* 6 and 32
- *Early Years Workbook 1*: pages 14-15
- *Letterland Phonics Online*: **Ff**

Other materials

- Toy firefighter's helmet (if available)
- Small magnets, pole and string
- Paper clips, paints and paper
- Toy fire engine or picture of one
- Shaving foam or hair-styling mousse

Teaching suggestions

Introducing Firefighter Fred

Show the children the picture of Firefighter Fred on page 17 of the *Letterland ABC Book* and introduce him using the sample script for **Session 1** (shown right) as a guide for what to say. Invite one or more children to find and touch Firefighter Fred on the *Alphabet Frieze*.

Firefighter Fred's letter shape

Introduce **Session 2**. Then sing or chant the handwriting verse shown below (on the *Handwriting Songs CD* or *Letterland Phonics Online)* to help teach Firefighter Fred's letter shape:

> First draw Fred's helmet.
> Then go down a way.
> Give him some arms
> and he'll put out the blaze.

Invite one or more children to finger trace Firefighter Fred's letter shape on the *ABC Book* or on both sides of the *Big Picture Code Card.*

Firefighter Fred's sound

'**Fff**...' is an *unvoiced* sound. Always whisper it to avoid saying 'f-uh'. Use Firefighter Fred's song on the *Alphabet Songs CD* or *Letterland Phonics Online* to achieve the correct sound.

Firefighter Fred's words

face	fix
fall	flag
farm	flame
fast	flower
favourite	fly
feel	fork
feet	four
fence	fox
fetch	friend
field	frog
fill	from
fireworks	fruit
fish	fun
five	funny

Firefighter Fred's sample script

Session 1: Introducing Firefighter Fred

Now we're going to meet **F**irefighter **F**red. **F**irefighter **F**red's a *very* busy man. What do you think he does? Quite right, he puts out **f**ires. Can you see that little bit of **f**ire? Can you see the **f**lames? He's got a big hosepipe that comes all the way from his **f**ire engine. And do you know, **F**irefighter **F**red doesn't just use water. He uses **f**oam to put out his **f**ires. *(You can demonstrate foam to the children using hair mousse!)*

Why do you think **F**irefighter **F**red wears a helmet? I think it's to protect his head when he's near a **f**ire, don't you?

Why do you think he wears boots on his **f**eet? Yes, I think it's to stop his **f**eet from getting wet in

Things to do

- **Being firefighters** Let everyone mime being firefighters putting out a big fire.
  [CD: Use their imagination in art and design...]

- **Counting fingers** Show how to count five fingers on each hand.
  [PSRN: Count reliably up to 10 everyday objects.]

- **Flame pictures** Help the children to make flame or fire pictures using red, yellow and orange finger paints and five fingers.
  [CD: Express and communicate their ideas...]

- **Follow my leader** Play Firefighter Fred's favourite game of 'Follow my leader'. Choose one child to be the leader and let him or her wear a firefighter's helmet, if available.
  [PSE: Be confident to try new activities...]

- **Fishing game** Cut out cardboard fish in different colours and sizes and add paper fasteners as eyes or paper clips as mouths. To make a rod, tie a length of string to a pole (e.g. bamboo) and tie the other end to a small magnet. The children can take it in turns to catch the fish. Then they can count them and talk about the colours and sizes of fish caught.
  [PSRN: Use language such as 'more' or 'less', 'greater' or 'smaller'...]

- **Further practice** Options for letter shapes:
  – *A-Z Copymasters:* **f** and **Ff**
  – *Early Years Handwriting Copymasters:* 6 and 32.
  For consolidation of both letter shape and sound use:
  – *Early Years Workbook 1*, pages 14-15.
  – *Letterland Phonics Online*.

Things to talk about

- **Fire engines** Talk about fire engines with the children, asking what they are for, why we need them and what they carry. Use a toy fire engine or the picture in the *ABC Book* to help. Can the children tell you why fire engines make a loud noise and have flashing lights?

- **Fred's foam** Bring some hair-styling mousse and squirt a small blob into each child's hand. Use it to explain how Firefighter Fred's foam acts like a blanket to put out a fire. (Ensure the children understand this is not real firefighting foam and they *must not* experiment with it!)

- **Fireworks** Discuss fireworks with the children and why they like them. Warn them not to touch fireworks. Tell them that Firefighter Fred always puts safety first and likes to make sure children never play with fire or fireworks.

- **Favourite foods** Talk about the children's favourite foods. Let them suggest Firefighter Fred's favourites, such as **fish fingers** and **fruit**.

- **Faces** Using a picture of Firefighter Fred, talk about faces and let the children name the different features.

Explaining the capital F shape

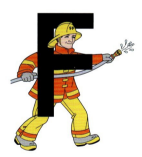

Ask the children to compare the small and capital **F** on the *Alphabet Frieze*. Let them tell you how the capital letter is the same and how it is different from Firefighter Fred's small letter shape.

---

the **f**oam. Can you remember our **f**irefighter's name? It's **F**irefighter **F**red. Can you say it with me? **F**irefighter **F**red.

Look! There's a little green **f**rog in this corner. He looks **f**rightened, doesn't he! **F**irefighter **F**red runs so **f**ast that the **f**rog has to jump **f**ast to get out of his way. Can anyone see another **f**rog near some **f**lowers?

Session 2: Firefighter Fred's shape and sound

Do you remember our **f**irefighter's name? Yes, it's **F**irefighter **F**red. Let's look how we make **F**irefighter **F**red's letter.

We start *right* at the top of his helmet and go *all* the way down, and then we go across his arms. Shall we try again? You go *right* down

from his helmet, *all* the way down and then we go *across* his arms. Where do we start writing **F**irefighter **F**red's letter? That's right. Right at the top of his helmet.

Can you remember how he puts out the **f**lames? With **fff**oam! And can you hear **F**irefighter **F**red's sound? '**Fff**..., **fff**...'.

Shall we say '**F**irefighter **F**red' together? Let's call him. '**F**irefighter **F**red, **F**irefighter **F**red!' Listen to his '**fff**...' sound as we call his name, '**F**irefighter **F**red.'

Can you see some other things that start with his '**fff**...' sound? Yes, we can see the **f**lames and the **f**oam. Let's ask him to put the **f**ire out. '**F**irefighter **F**red, please put the **f**ire out with your **f**oam.'

Golden Girl

Objective

To teach the letter shapes and sound for **g** and **G**.

What you need

Letterland materials

- *Big Picture Code Cards*: Golden Girl
- *A-Z Copymasters*: **g** and **Gg**
- *Early Years Handwriting Copymasters*: *7* and *33*
- *Early Years Workbook 2*: pages 2-3
- *Letterland Phonics Online*: **Gg**

Other materials

- Items for a miniature garden
- Pictures of flowers
- Coloured paper
- Icing sugar
- Green food colouring
- Green grapes (if possible)
- Gloves, including gardening gloves

Teaching suggestions

Introducing Golden Girl

Show the children the picture of Golden Girl on page 19 of the *Letterland ABC Book* and introduce her using the sample script for **Session 1** (shown right) as a guide for what to say. Invite one or more children to find and touch Golden Girl on the *Letterland Alphabet Frieze*. Ask them to touch her green clothes and her glasses (which she wears for reading).

Golden Girl's letter shape

Introduce **Session 2**. Then sing or chant the handwriting verse shown below (on the *Handwriting Songs CD* or *Letterland Phonics Online*) to help teach Golden Girl's shape:

Go round Golden Girl's head.
Go down her golden hair.
Then curve to make her swing
so she can sit there.

Invite one or more children to finger trace Golden Girl's letter shape on the *ABC Book* or on both sides of the *Big Picture Code Card,* and also to find her go-cart on the frieze.

Golden Girl's sound

Ask the children to *start* saying Golden Girl's name and they will find her sound in the back of their throats. (If you have a George or Gemma in your group, explain that Golden Girl sometimes gives her good friend 'Gentle Ginger' a turn in her go-cart and her swing.) Practise with Golden Girl's song on the *Alphabet Songs CD* or *Phonics Online.*

Golden Girl's words

garden	golden
get	goldfish
giggle	good
girl	grandfather
give	grandmother
glasses	grapes
glue	grass
go	green
goat	grow

Golden Girl sample script

Session 1: Introducing Golden Girl

Who's swinging on this swing? That's right, it's a **g**irl – a **g**irl with long **g**olden hair. Do you think she likes swinging? Yes, I think she does, because she's smiling while she swings. We call her **G**olden **G**irl because of her **g**olden hair. Can you say her name with me? **G**olden **G**irl!

I *do* like **G**olden **G**irl's **g**arden. Look at that lovely **g**reen **g**rass.

Oh! She'd better close her **g**reenhouse door. Can you see an animal with **g**rey horns outside the **g**reenhouse? That's **G**olden **G**irl's **g**oat. **G**oats **g**obble up anything – even shoes if you leave them lying around! And they do love **g**reen **g**rapes.

Things to do

- **Miniature garden** Help the children to grow a miniature garden, either using real garden materials, such as grass seed, moss, cress, flowers etc., or by making flowers out of modelling dough.
  [KU: Investigate objects and materials...]

- **Things in the garden** Go out into a garden together, if possible, and look for items beginning with Golden Girl's sound, such as a gate, grass, grey and green things, ground, gravel, grit and greenhouse.
  [KU: Investigate objects and materials...]

- **Gorgeous garden picture** Help the children to create a 'gorgeous garden' picture by filling a large sheet of paper from edge to edge with drawings of flowers. Alternatively, the children could make one using pictures of flowers cut out from magazines or seed catalogues. They can then give it as a gift to someone at home.
  [CD: Express and communicate their ideas, thoughts and feelings...]

- **Cookery** Help the children to add green icing to biscuits, or let them sample some green grapes.
  [CD: Explore colour, texture, shape...]

- **Further practice** Options for letter shapes:
  – *Lower Case Pictogram Copymasters:* **g** and **Gg**
  – *Early Years Handwriting Copymasters:* 7 and 33.
  For consolidation of both letter shape and sound use:
  – *Early Years Workbook 2*, pages 2-3.
  – *Letterland Phonics Online*.

Things to talk about

- **Favourite colours** Talk about the children's favourite colours. Show them some green, yellow, silver and gold paper or other items. Which colours might Golden Girl like best? (The ones beginning with her sound.)

- **Wearing glasses** Ask if anyone wears or knows someone else who wears glasses, and talk about how glasses can help us.

- **Gloves** Show the children different kinds of gloves and mittens. Look at how many places each kind has for fingers. Talk about how gardening gloves differ from other gloves.

- **Giving gifts** Golden Girl loves giving grapes from her garden to all her friends. Discuss giving gifts.

- **Knowing why** Reminder: see page 19.

Explaining the capital G sound

When Golden Girl is needed to start an important word, she gets out of her swing and gets into her go-cart. On her swing she is not looking in the Reading Direction, but when she is in her go-cart she has to look where she is going so that she does not bump into the other Letterland characters. She always uses her go-cart letter shape to start her name, Golden Girl. She makes her usual 'g...' sound as she goes.

Let's warn **G**olden **G**irl about the goat. '**G**olden **G**irl, you'd better close your **g**reenhouse door so your **g**oat doesn't **g**obble up your **g**rapes.' Can you call her again? '**G**olden **G**irl.'

Session 2: Golden Girl's shape and sound

Can you remember *this* **g**irl's name? Yes, it's **G**olden **G**irl. She has **g**olden hair. While she swings we hear the sound, '**g**..., **g**..., **g**...' for **G**olden **G**irl.

This swing is an unusual one. Look, this piece goes *round* her head and then there's a gently curving piece for her to sit on.

I'm going to draw her swing now. Start at the top, go *round* her head, *up* to the rope, *down* and curve *round* to make a swing. Let's do it again while we say her '**g**...' sound. Go round her head,

up to the rope, down and curve round to make her **g**arden swing.

Can you see **G**olden **G**irl's **g**arden **g**ate? Why should **G**olden **G**irl keep her **g**arden **g**ate shut? Yes, if she left it open her **g**oat might **g**o through the **g**ate and **g**et lost.

I can see a **g**reenhouse with **g**rapes **g**rowing in it. I'm **g**lad that **G**olden **G**irl's swing is not too near the **g**reenhouse, because **g**reenhouses are made of **g**...! What are **g**reenhouses made of? Yes, **g**reenhouses are made of **g**lass, and **g**lass breaks very easily.

Sometimes **G**olden **G**irl **g**ets out of her swing and **g**ets into her **g**o-cart. Look at her **g**oing fast in her **g**o-cart. She *always* uses her **g**o-cart letter to start her name, **G**olden **G**irl.

Harry Hat Man

Objective

To teach the letter shapes and sound for **h** and **H**.

What you need

Letterland materials

- *Big Picture Code Cards*: Harry Hat Man
- *A-Z Copymasters*: **h** and **Hh**
- *Early Years Handwriting Copymasters*: 8 and 34
- *Early Years Workbook 2*: pages 4-5
- *Letterland Phonics Online*: **Hh**

Other materials

- One or more boxes
- Paper, paints and crayons
- As many hats as possible

Teaching suggestions

Introducing Harry Hat Man

Show the children the picture of Harry Hat Man on page 21 of the *Letterland ABC Book* and introduce him using the sample script for **Session 1** (shown right) as a guide for what to say. Invite one or more children to hop over to the *Letterland Alphabet Frieze* and touch Harry Hat Man's head and his heels. Explain the capital H shape if asked (see opposite).

Harry Hat Man's letter shape

Introduce **Session 2**. Then sing or chant the handwriting verse shown below (on the *Handwriting Songs CD* or *Letterland Phonics Online*) to help teach Harry Hat Man's letter shape:

Hurry from the Hat Man's head
down to his heel on the ground.
Go up and bend his knee over,
so he'll hop while he makes his sound.

Invite one or more children to finger trace Harry Hat Man's letter shape on the *Letterland ABC Book* or on both sides of the *Big Picture Code Card*.

Harry Hat Man's sound

This sound is really a little sigh, or panting sound, to be whispered. Make sure nobody adds voice, turning '**hhh**...' into 'huh'. That hurts the Hat Man's ears! Practise with Harry Hat Man's song on the *Alphabet Songs CD* or *Letterland Phonics Online*.

Harry Hat Man's words

ham	hill
hand	his
happy	holly
hat	home
hear	honey
hedge	horrible
hedgehog	horse
helicopter	hot
helpful	house
hen	how
her	huge
here	hungry

Harry Hat Man's sample script

Session 1: Introducing Harry Hat Man

I can see **H**arry **H**at Man. Do you like his **h**at? It's a very **h**airy **h**at, isn't it? **H**arry **H**at Man *always* wears that green **h**airy **h**at on his **h**ead. He wouldn't go anywhere without it!

Harry **H**at Man is carrying a bundle of **h**ay. Do you think it's for his **h**orse? He's **h**olding **h**is other **h**and up. I think he's waving '**h**ello' to us! Let's all wave '**h**ello' to him. Put your **h**and up, ready? All together, '**H**ello, **H**arry **H**at Man!'

Oh dear. I forgot! The **H**arry **H**at Man **h**ates noise, so we had better do that again much more quietly. Let's call out in a whisper: '**H**ello, **H**arry **H**at Man.' Ah, lovely and quiet. That's *exactly* how the **H**at Man likes it.

I can see **H**arry **H**at Man's **h**ouse on the **h**ill.

Things to do

- **Hand play** The children put their hands on their head, heel, hip, other hand, hair and heart, in any order that you say. End with everyone holding hands.
  [CLL: Extend their vocabulary, exploring...]

- **Harry Hat Man picture** Together, make a huge picture of Harry Hat Man and then display it. Get the children to make hand-prints on small pieces of paper, then cut them out, label them and display them around the picture. Add pictures of other objects starting with the Hat Man's sound.
  [CLL: Hear and say initial and final sounds...]

- **Hunt the hat** Hide a picture of Harry Hat Man's hat and choose a child to look for it. Say 'Warmer, warmer' as the child gets nearer to the hiding place, and 'Hot!' when he or she is beside it.
  [PSE: Respond to significant experiences...]

- **Hopping** Divide the children into two groups. Let one group hop towards the other group, who stand listening to the panting 'hhh...' sounds of the children hopping towards them. Now repeat with roles reversed.
  [PD: Recognise the changes that happen...]

- **Further practice** Options for letter shapes:
  – *A-Z Copymasters:* **h** and **Hh**
  – *Early Years Handwriting Copymasters:* 8 and 34.
  For consolidation of both letter shape and sound use:
  – *Early Years Workbook 2,* pages 4-5.
  – *Letterland Phonics Online.*

Things to talk about

- **Hats** Ask the children to bring in all kinds of hats and use those collected in 'Clever Cat's Costume Box', (see **Dressing up** on page 17). Talk about who would wear them, and why.

- **Horrible noise** Ask if any child hates noise and if they know anyone else who also hates noise, perhaps their parents or teacher. Do they think that they are sometimes too noisy? Stress consideration for other people.

- **Houses and homes** Talk about the Hat Man's unusual house using page 23 of the *ABC Book*, and let the children compare it with their own homes. Talk about what homes are made from and look at those of various animals, e.g. a dog kennel, bird cage or nest, fox den, rabbit hutch or burrow, etc.

- **Helping hands** Talk about how our hands help us and then try using just one. Discuss how we can use our hands to help others, such as helping at home by tidying up, etc.

Explaining the capital H shape

Tell the children that when Harry Hat Man has a chance to start a name, he is so happy that he does a handstand with his hat on! To write his capital letter, children need to start up at the Hat Man's heel, going from heel to hand, and heel to hand. Then they can draw the line across.

But there's something odd about his **h**ouse. What's that on top of it? It looks more like a green **h**airy **h**at than a roof!

My **h**ouse has a roof on it. Does your **h**ouse have a roof on it as well? **H**arry **H**at Man's **h**ouse has a **h**at for a roof! I wonder **h**ow that **h**appened, don't you?

Let's all wave goodbye to **H**arry **H**at Man now. We'll be meeting him again soon.

Session 2: Harry Hat Man's shape and sound

Can you think why our friend here has no shoes on? It's because he **h**ates noise.

Too much noise gives him a **h**orrible **h**eadache, so he doesn't even wear shoes because shoes make too much noise as he **h**ops along.

When the **H**arry **H**at Man goes into a word, do you know what sound he makes? You have to whisper it, like this: '**hhh**...'. Can you **h**ear it at the start of his name? **Hhh**arry **Hhh**at Man. Did you **h**ear that '**hhh**...' sound at the beginning of his name?

Watch while we make **H**arry **H**at Man's letter. We start at his **h**ead and go *down* his long back, right to his **h**eel. Then we go back up *over* his knee and stop at his other **h**eel. Let's do it again and whisper his '**hhh**...' sound as we start at his **h**ead ..., go *down* to his **h**eel..., go up *over* his knee... and down to his other **h**eel. Remember, **H**arry **H**at Man says '**hhh**...'.

What can we see in the sky? It isn't a plane. You're quite right, it's a **h**elicopter.

Harry **H**at Man is **h**appy that the **h**elicopter is **h**urrying off. Helicopters are noisy and what does the **H**arry **H**at Man **h**ate? Noise! That's why he **h**imself never speaks above a whisper, '**hhh**...'.

Impy Ink

Objectives

To teach the letter shapes for **i** and **I** and the short vowel sound 'ĭ...', and to introduce briefly the long vowel's name, 'ī...'.

What you need

Letterland materials

- *Big Picture Code Cards*: Impy Ink and Mr I
- *A-Z Copymasters*: **i** and **Ii**
- *Early Years Handwriting Copymasters*: 9 and 35
- *Early Years Workbook 2*: pages 6-7
- *Letterland Phonics Online*: **Ii**

Other materials

- Pictures of insects
- Bottle of ink
- Ball-point pen
- Rubber stamps
- Ink pad
- Paint and card

Teaching suggestions

Introducing Impy Ink

Before introducing the short 'ĭ...' sound, it is a good idea to revise the short 'ă...' and 'ĕ...' sounds. Then show the children the picture of Impy Ink on page 23 of the *ABC Book* and introduce him using the sample script for **Session 1** (shown right) as a guide for what to say. Invite one or more children to find Impy Ink and the ink pen on the *Alphabet Frieze*. Talk briefly about Mr I, the Ice Cream Man, too, if asked (see opposite).

Impy Ink's letter shape

Introduce **Session 2**. Then sing or chant the handwriting verse shown below (on the *Handwriting Songs CD* or *Letterland Phonics Online*) to help teach Impy Ink's letter shape:

**Inside the ink bottle draw a line.
Add an inky dot. That's fine!**

Invite one or more children to finger trace Impy Ink's letter shape on the *Letterland ABC Book* or on both sides of the *Big Picture Code Card*.

Impy Ink's sound

Tell the children just to *start* saying 'Impy Ink' to find his little 'ĭ...' sound. See who can hear his sound in their name, either at the start or inside it. Impy Ink's song on the *Alphabet Songs CD* or on *Letterland Phonics Online* will help in pronouncing his sound correctly.

Impy Ink's words

if	inside
ill	interesting
important	into
in	invitation
infants	itch
ink	internet
insect	igloo

Impy Ink sample script

Session 1: Introducing Impy Ink

I can see a very special bottle on this page. Do you know what's in this bottle? It's something called **i**nk. **I**nk bottles usually only have one colour of **i**nk in them. But *this* bottle has rainbow coloured **i**nk in it. That makes it really special! You can pour **i**nk. You can pour it out of the bottle. We keep **i**nk in a bottle because otherwise it would spill and make a *terrible* mess!

In Letterland, all the school children use special **i**nk pens to write with. Can you see a special rainbow **i**nk pen in this picture? The Letterland children dip their pens **i**nto their **i**nk bottles and fill them up with **i**nk so they can write with them.

Things to do

- **Insect pictures** Collect pictures of insects. Help to make insect pictures as well, using different coloured paint blobs; add six legs, or eight for spiders.
  [KU: Look closely at similarities, differences...]

- **Ink** Bring in a real bottle of ink to show the children. Also show them the ink stem in a plastic ball-point pen. Let them use an ink pad to press rubber stamp pictures on to paper. They could also crumple up newspapers and look at their hands afterwards. Explain that it is ink that makes them dirty.
  [KU: Investigate objects and materials...]

- **Invitations** Help the children to make invitation cards asking their favourite Letterlanders to tea. Talk about what they would say to, or ask, their guests.
  [PSE: Understand that people have different needs...]

- **Further practice** Options for letter shapes:
  – *A-Z Copymasters:* **i** and **Ii**
  – *Early Years Handwriting Copymasters:* 9 and 35.
  For consolidation of both letter shape and sound use:
  – *Early Years Workbook 2*, pages 6-7.
  – *Letterland Phonics Online*.

Things to talk about

- **Introductions** Make a game of introducing each other. Ask each child to say one or two things about another child, such as, 'His/Her name is..., he/she lives near..., has a baby brother, likes..., his/her favourite food (game, song) is...', etc. Extend the game by asking the children to introduce themselves – or even you!

- **Important things** Talk about things that are important, such as safety, kindness, brushing teeth (cleanliness), and also things that are important in the children's personal lives, such as grandparents coming, etc.

- **Interesting things** Use the word '**interesting**' as often as possible while you focus on this Letterlander and his sound.

Explaining the capital I shape

Explain that when Impy Ink takes a deep breath, his letter gets so tall and thin that you can't see his ink spot any more. His letter looks like his ink pen instead.

Introducing Mr I, the Ice Cream Man

Show the children the picture of Mr I, the Ice Cream Man, on either the *Letterland Alphabet Frieze* or on the *Big Picture Code Cards*. Explain that Mr I is a very important person in Letterland because he sells ink and ice cream, and that at times he also says his name 'ī...' in words.

Mr I's words

I
ice cream
idea
iron
island
ivy

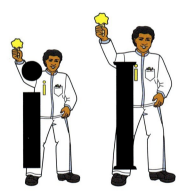

Can you see, there's a smiling face on this bottle of ink? That face belongs to Impy Ink. Can you say his name for me? Impy Ink. That's right. Impy Ink lives in the Letterland school.

If anyone wants to fill their ink pen with rainbow ink, we take the top off Impy Ink, put the ink pen into his ink and fill the pen up.

Let's pretend to dip the ink pen into Impy Ink's bottle while we say his name: Impy Ink.

Session 2: Impy Ink's shape and sound

Can you remember who this is on this page? Yes, it's Impy Ink. Impy Ink makes an 'ĭ...' sound. Let's say it while we pretend to put the ink pen into Impy Ink. 'ĭ..., ĭ..., ĭ...'.

Look at Impy Ink's letter. To write his letter I go *straight* down his bottle and then I put a dot on top. Can you do it with me? Start at the top, go *straight* down and put his dot on top. Then we say, 'ĭ...' for Impy Ink. Can you say it for me? Impy Ink says 'ĭ..., ĭ...'.

Now let's say it together while we draw his letter. Start at the top, go *down* his letter, put a dot on top and say 'ĭ..., ĭ...'.

I can see two mini-beasts who should not be near the ink. Can you see them at the bottom of the page? They are insects.

Insects have six legs. If they put their legs in the wet ink, they will make ink marks all across the page. I think we ought to move those insects away from Impy Ink, don't you! Otherwise there will be ink marks everywhere.

Jumping Jim

Objective

To teach the letter shapes and sound for **j** and **J**.

What you need

Letterland materials

- *Big Picture Code Cards*: Jumping Jim
- *A-Z Copymasters*: **j** and **Jj**
- *Early Years Handwriting Copymasters*: 10 and 36
- *Early Years Workbook 2*: pages 8-9
- *Letterland Phonics Online*: **Jj**

Other materials

- Pieces of different coloured green paper
- Large box
- Coffee jar lids
- Jam, jelly or fruit juice
- Paper, paints and crayons
- Old greetings cards
- Envelopes
- Jack-in-a-box (if available)

Jumping Jim's sound

To say Jumping Jim's sound correctly, ask the children just to start saying his name and they will find his sound pushing itself out of their mouths. Practise with Jim's song on the *Alphabet Songs CD* or on *Letterland Phonics Online*.

Jumping Jim's words

jacket	journey
jam	joy
January	jug
jar	juggle
jaw	juice
jelly	July
jigsaw	jump
job	jumper
jog	June
joke	jungle
jolly	just

Teaching suggestions

Introducing Jumping Jim

Show the children the picture of Jumping Jim on page 25 of the *ABC Book* and introduce him using the sample script for **Session 1** (shown right) as a guide for what to say. Invite one or more children to find and touch Jumping Jim on the *Alphabet Frieze*.

Jumping Jim's letter shape

Introduce **Session 2**. Sing or chant the handwriting verse shown below (on the *Handwriting Songs CD* or *Letterland Phonics Online*) to help teach Jumping Jim's letter shape:

Just draw down Jim, bending his knees.
Then add the one ball which everyone sees.

Invite one or more children to finger trace Jumping Jim's letter shape on the *Letterland ABC Book* or on both sides of the *Big Picture Code Cards*.

Jumping Jim sample script

Session 1: Introducing Jumping Jim

Before I get my book out, we're all going to stand up. Now we're going to make three **j**umps. Ready? We're going to **j**ump now: **j**ump... and another one, **j**ump... and another one, **j**ump.... Oh, well done! That's *three* big **j**umps. Now if we sit down *very, very* carefully and rest our **j**umping feet, I've got a picture to show you. Are you all ready?

Look at my picture. What's *this* boy doing? Yes, he's **j**umping as well. What a big **j**ump he's making. He's **j**umping all the way through Letterland! I'll tell you his name. His name is **J**umping **J**im. Can you say it for me? **J**umping **J**im. That's right. **J**umping **J**im **j**umps through Letterland, **j**ust like we've been **j**umping.

Jumping **J**im does something else that's very,

Things to do

- **Jumping Jim's jungle** Show the children how to tear pieces of green paper into leaves. Join the leaves into leaf chains and hang them from the ceiling for a jungle effect.
  [CD: Explore colour, texture, shape...]

- **Junk box** Label a 'Junk Box' and encourage everyone to collect oddments. Use it now and in the future for junk modelling.
  [CLL: Link sounds to letters...]

- **Jim's jeep** Ask the children to draw, paint or make a junk model jeep for Jumping Jim. Stick coffee jar lids on to the jeep for wheels.
  [KU: Build and construct with a wide range...]

- **Jim's jet** Help to make model jet planes using junk from the Junk Box (see above).
  [KU: Build and construct with a wide range...]

- **Food tasting** Have a jam, jelly or juice tasting and let the children decide on their favourites.
  [KU: Investigate objects and materials...]

- **Jumps** Let the children play at being Jumping Jims. Set up jumps in the playground for jumping over, or items for jumping off.
  [PD: Move with confidence, imagination...]

- **Jigsaws** Help the children to make their own jigsaw puzzles. Let them draw a picture, or use old greeting cards, then cut them into four, five or six pieces. They can then try putting the jigsaw pieces back together again. They may like to take their jigsaw home in an envelope to reassemble there.
  [KU: Look closely at similarities, differences...]

- **Further practice** Options for letter shapes:
  – *Lower Case Pictogram Copymasters:* **j** and **Jj**
  – *A-Z Copymasters:* 10 and 36.
  For consolidation of both letter shape and sound use:
  – *Early Years Workbook 2*, pages 8-9.
  – *Letterland Phonics Online.*

Things to talk about

- **Months of the year** Ask everyone to listen carefully as you recite the months of the year and get them to raise their hands when they hear a month starting with Jumping Jim's sound (**January**, **June** and **July**).

- **Jack-in-a-box** Find out if a child has a Jack-in-the-box that they can bring in to show everybody, or provide one yourself.

- **Journeys** Talk about long and short journeys with the children, perhaps to the shops, to visit relatives, etc. Ask what Jumping Jim would need to take with him on a long journey (**jeans**, **jumpers**, etc.), or where he might go to (**Japan**, **Jamaica**, **Jerusalem**, etc.).

- **Knowing why** Reminder: see page 19.

Explaining the capital J shape

In Letterland, whenever Jumping Jim is needed to start an important word, he is so pleased that he does a big jump and his head disappears in the clouds. Then we can't see his ball any more.

---

very clever. Can you see what he has in his hand? Yes, he has a ball. But **J**umping **J**im doesn't throw **j**ust one ball. He can sometimes throw three balls all together – one, two, three. Does anybody know what that's called? It's called **j**uggling. And **J**umping **J**im can **j**uggle. He can throw three balls up in the air and catch another ball at the same time!

I find it hard to throw *one* ball up into the air and catch it. I can't throw three balls up and catch them all – one, two, three. But **J**umping **J**im can. Let's say his name as he **j**uggles those balls. **J**umping **J**im. That's right.

Session 2: Jumping Jim's shape and sound

Can you remember who this is? Yes, it's **J**umping **J**im. He can **j**ump and **j**uggle. Do you know what sound **J**umping **J**im makes when he **j**umps into words? **J**ust start to say his name, '**J**...'. Yes, **J**umping **J**im says, '**j**...' at the beginning of his

name and in words like **j**ump and **j**uggle. Let's say his sound while we draw him.

We start **j**ust under **J**umping **J**im's hand where he's holding the ball. We go *all* the way down his leg and *round* to his **j**umping shoes. Shall we try it again? Start at his hand where he's holding the ball, go *all* the way down his leg and *round* to his **j**umping shoes. And don't forget to give him a spot for a little **j**umping **j**uggling ball. Let's do it again and this time we will say '**j**...' for **J**umping **J**im.

Sometimes he **j**umps so high you can't see his ball. It's hidden by the clouds. **J**ust look. There's something else in those clouds. Can you see a plane in the clouds?

I wonder what sort of plane it is. If it belongs to **J**umping **J**im it will start with his special '**j**...' sound. That's right. It's a **j**et plane in the sky above **J**umping **J**im.

Kicking King

Objective

To teach the letter shapes and sound for **k** and **K**.

What you need

Letterland materials

- *Big Picture Code Cards*: Kicking King
- *A-Z Copymasters*: **k** and **Kk**
- *Early Years Handwriting Copymasters*: 11 and 36
- *Early Years Workbook 2*: pages 10-11
- *Letterland Phonics Online*: **Kk**

Other materials

- Coloured paper or card
- Gummed paper
- Tin foil
- Newspaper
- Tray or wide box
- Kaleidoscope
- Old magazines or catalogues
- Kiwi fruit or tin of fruit including kiwi slices
- Bag of sugar, or something 1 kilo weight
- Bathroom scales (if available)

Teaching suggestions

Introducing Kicking King

Show the children the picture of Kicking King on page 27 of the *ABC Book* and introduce him using the sample script for **Session 1** (shown right) as a guide. Invite one or more children to find and touch Kicking King on the *Alphabet Frieze*. They could also touch his arm and his kicking foot.

Kicking King's letter shape

Introduce **Session 2**. Then sing or chant the handwriting verse shown below (as on the *Handwriting Songs CD* or *Phonics Online*) to help teach Kicking King's letter shape:

Kicking King's body is a straight stick.
Add his arm, then his leg, so he can kick!

Invite one or more children to finger trace Kicking King's letter shape on the *ABC Book* or on both sides of the *Big Picture Code Card*.

Kicking King's sound

Explain that Kicking King and Clever Cat are very pleased that they both make exactly the same sound in words. The king is too busy looking after the kingdom to appear in many words, so he is glad that Clever Cat can do the job in most words. Kicking King's song on the *Alphabet Songs CD* or *Letterland Phonics Online* will help in teaching the correct sound.

Kicking King's words

kaleidoscope	kid
kangaroo	kilo
keep	kind
kennel	king
ketchup	kiss
kettle	kitchen
key	kite
kick	kitten

Kicking King sample script

Session 1: Introducing Kicking King

I can see a **k**ing on this page. How do I know that he is a **k**ing? Yes, he's wearing a crown on his head, but this is an unusual **k**ing. Just look at his feet! What's he doing? He's **k**icking a ball.

Our **k**ing loves playing football. He loves **k**icking that ball. That's why we call him **K**icking **K**ing. But do you know, he's a very **k**ind **k**ing as well. And because he is a very **k**ind **k**ing, he only ever **k**icks footballs. I'm pleased about that.

There's an animal on this page. I think he wants to join in the football game as well, because he

Things to do

- **King's crowns** Hand out strips of paper with a zig-zag edge for the children to decorate as Kicking King's crowns, perhaps with pieces of coloured gummed paper or foil. Then staple them together for the children to wear.
  [CD: Use their imagination in art and design...]

- **Kicking balls** Show how to make paper balls out of screwed up newspaper. Take turns trying to kick the balls into a tray or wide box. See how many balls are in the box and practise counting 0, 1, 2, 3, etc.
  [PD: Show awareness of space, of themselves...]

- **Kite pictures** Draw kite shapes on the top half of some pieces of paper. On the bottom half, the children can draw Kicking King, then add lines from the kites to his hand.
  [CD: Explore colour, texture, shape...]

- **Kaleidoscope** Take turns viewing through a kaleidoscope. Explain that Kicking King loves looking through one, too.
  [CD: Explore colour, texture, shape...]

- **Kitchen collage** Help to make a kitchen collage, using pictures cut out of magazines or catalogues.
  [PD: Handle tools, objects, construction...]

- **Kiwi fruit** Bring in fresh kiwi fruit for the children to share, or tinned fruit with kiwi slices.
  [CD: Respond in a variety of ways...]

- **Further practice** Options for letter shapes:
  - A-Z Copymasters: **k** and **Kk**
  - Early Years Handwriting Copymasters: 11 and 36.
  For consolidation of both letter shape and sound use:
  - Early Years Workbook 2, pages 10-11.
  - Letterland Phonics Online.

Things to talk about

- **Kittens** In Letterland, Kicking King keeps his **kittens** in his **kitchen**. Ask if anyone has a kitten and where they keep it.

- **Kindness** Talk about kindness and explain that the King is a kind king who is kind to people and to animals, especially his **kittens**, pet **kangaroo**, and **koala bear**. Ask who is kind to the children, and how they can be kind, for instance, to each other, to brothers and sisters and to pets.

- **Kangaroo, koala and kookaburra** Talk about all these creatures from Australia and show pictures of them, if available. You could also sing the song 'Kookaburra sits in the old gum tree'.

- **Kilo** Bring in some objects, such as a bag of sugar, to show how heavy a kilo is. Ask the children to see if they can find out at home how many kilos they weigh. Alternatively, bring in some scales and weigh each child.

- **Names** Find out if any of the children have, or know someone with, a first or surname beginning with Kicking King's letter, such as **Kate**, **Katie**, **Katherine**, **Kevin**, **Khaleda**, etc.

- **Rhyme** If available, read Kicking King's poem, from the Alphabet of Rhymes Book, page 11.

Explaining the capital K shape

Tell the children that when Kicking King starts an important word, he takes a deep breath. His arm and kicking leg then get longer so he will look more important in that word.

is very good at **k**icking too. Do you know what animal he is? He's a very unusual animal. He has huge, long back legs and very short front legs. He's a **k**angaroo.

Kangaroos like **k**icking. I think this **k**angaroo is going to help our **K**icking **K**ing play football. 'Don't **k**ick **K**icking **K**ing, **k**angaroo, will you!'

Session 2: Kicking King's shape and sound

I think you've remembered who this is. Yes, it's **K**icking **K**ing. Can you say **K**icking **K**ing's sound for me? It's '**k**...' for **k**ick and '**k**...' for **k**ing. Let's say it together. **K**icking **K**ing says, '**k**..., **k**...'. And when we draw him, we start *right* by his neck. We

go *down* to his foot and then we *start* by his hand, go *in* to his waist and *out* to his **k**icking foot.

Shall we do that again? Start by his head, go *right* down to his foot. Start by his hand, go to his waist and out to his **k**icking foot. Let's say his sound again, '**k**..., **k**...' for **K**icking **K**ing.

Can you see the king's **k**ittens playing at the bottom of the page? And there's a bird perching on a **k**ettle just in front of the **k**ennel. That bird is called a **k**ingfisher. The **k**angaroo and the **k**ittens and the **k**ingfisher are all **K**icking **K**ing's pets. They love him because he is always so **k**ind to them. Can you see any other animals in the picture whose name begins with **K**icking **K**ing's letter?

Lucy Lamp Light

Objective

To teach the letter shapes and sound for **l** and **L**.

What you need

Letterland materials

- *Big Picture Code Cards*: Lucy Lamp Light
- *A-Z Copymasters*: **l** and **Ll**
- *Early Years Handwriting Copymasters*: 12 and 37
- *Early Years Workbook 2*: pages 12-13
- *Letterland Phonics Online*: **Ll**

Other materials

- Envelopes
- Paper and pens
- Old cotton reels
- White cotton wool
- Pipe cleaners
- Lettuce
- Lemonade
- Lemons
- Leeks
- Lentils
- Labels (luggage ones, if available)
- Various leaves
- Torch
- Bicycle lamp
- Other types of lights (if available)

Teaching suggestions

Introducing Lucy Lamp Light

Show the children the picture of Lucy Lamp Light on page 29 of the *ABC Book* and introduce her using the sample script for **Session 1** (shown right) as a guide for what to say. Invite one or more children to find and touch Lucy Lamp Light on the *Alphabet Frieze*. If asked, talk briefly about her capital letter shape, too (see opposite).

Lucy Lamp Light's letter shape

Introduce **Session 2**. Then sing or chant the handwriting verse shown below (as on *Handwriting Songs CD* or *Letterland Phonics Online*) to help teach Lucy Lamp Light's letter shape:

> Lucy looks like one long line.
> Go straight from head to foot
> and she's ready to shine!

Invite a child to finger trace down Lucy's long straight letter on the *Letterland ABC Book* or on both sides of the *Big Picture Code Card*.

Lucy Lamp Light's sound

The best way to avoid adding an unwanted 'uh' sound to '**lll**...' is to keep the tip of your tongue touching the roof of your mouth. This will make blending sounds much easier: not 'lluh-eg' but '**llleg**' for **leg**. Lucy Lamp Light's song on the *Alphabet Songs CD* or *Letterland Phonics Online* will help in achieving the correct sound.

Lucy Lamp Light's words

ladder	lemon	look
lamb	letter	lost
lamp	lighthouse	lots
large	like	lovely
laugh	little	lunch
leaf	lion	
left	live	
leg	long	

Lucy Lamp Light sample script

Session 1: Introducing Lucy Lamp Light

Look at this **l**ovely tall **l**ady. She's called **L**ucy **L**amp **L**ight. See that hat on her head. It's like a **l**amp shade, isn't it? And there's **l**ight coming from her **l**ovely face, just like the **l**ight from a **l**amp. It **l**ights up all the animals that come near her.

Look, there's a **l**ittle **l**amb..., some **l**izards..., a **l**eopard on a tree trunk... and behind him a **ll**ama. And what's that big animal **l**ying down behind **L**ucy? Yes, it's a **l**ion with its **l**ittle **l**ion cub. Even a **l**obster has joined them to enjoy **L**ucy's **l**ovely **l**emon coloured **l**ight.

Things to do

- **Leaping up** Play 'Lucy Lamp Light says: Leap up! ' Start with everyone crouching down as low as they can. Then the children all leap up into the air and try to be long and thin like Lucy.
[PSRN: Use language such as 'more' or 'less', 'greater' or 'smaller'...]

- **Letters** Provide paper and envelopes for the children to write letters to Lucy, or to other friends and relatives.
[CLL: Attempt writing for various purposes...]

- **Little lambs** Make some little lambs together using cotton reels covered in cotton wool. Give them pipe cleaner legs.
[CD: Explore colour, texture, shape...]

- **Lunch** For lunch, eat or drink as many things as possible beginning with Lucy's sound, such as lettuce and lemonade. The children could also look at lemons, leeks and lentils.
[KU: Investigate objects and materials by using all of their senses...]

- **Labels** Help the children to make labels for various objects in the classroom, starting with those beginning with the letter **l** (e.g. light switch, library books, lockers etc.) If available, use luggage labels.
[CLL: Use their phonic knowledge to write simple regular words...]

- **Further practice** Options for letter shapes:
  – *A-Z Copymasters:* **l** and **Ll**
  – *Early Years Handwriting Copymasters:* 12 and 37.
For consolidation of both letter shape and sound use:
  – *Early Years Workbook 2,* pages 12-13.
  – *Letterland Phonics Online.*

Things to talk about

- **Length** Talk about length to the children and ask how long their left hand is. Let each child in turn (so that everyone is watching) measure something with their hand and say how many hands long it is. See who has the longest hand in the room.

- **Leaf display** Make a collection of leaves. Talk about their different shapes and colours and compare the fronts and backs. Use them to make a leaf display around a brown paper tree.

- **Lights** Bring in a torch, a bicycle lamp and any other lights. Talk about why we need traffic lights, street lights, lighthouses, etc.

- **Ladders** Talk about the people who might use a ladder, such as decorators (painting a house), builders, window cleaners, firefighters, etc.

- **Ladybirds** Talk about ladybirds, what they look like, how many spots they have, and what they like to eat (tiny flies).

Explaining the capital L shape

Explain that whenever Lucy Lamp Light starts important words, she takes a deep breath and gets bigger. In her case, however, her legs also grow  longer, so long in fact, that she has to kneel with her legs on the line. If you can, take a photograph of all the children kneeling in a line miming Lucy in her capital letter position. Display the photograph by the lighthouse.

Look in the distance. There is a tall, thin building. It's a lighthouse, and that's where Lucy Lamp Light lives. You only find lighthouses by the sea, and they always have a light on top, like this one. When ships are a long way out at sea, lighthouses help them to find their way towards the land. Can you say Lucy Lamp Light's name with me? Lucy Lamp Light.

Session 2: Lucy Lamp Light's shape and sound

Do you remember the name of this lovely lady? Yes, her name is Lucy Lamp Light. Let's say her name together: Lucy Lamp Light. She makes a 'lll...' sound. Listen, Lucy Lamp Light says 'lll...'. Can you say that with me? Lucy Lamp Light says 'lll..., lll...'.

Do you remember the names of these animals? What's the biggest one called? That's right! It's a lion! Can you hear Lucy's 'lll...' sound in the word lion? And 'lll...' in Lucy Lamp Light's name?

Let's see if we can make Lucy Lamp Light's letter. It's so easy! It starts *right* at the top under her chin and just goes *straight* down to her feet. It's just one long line. You try with me. Start at her chin and go straight down to her feet. Curve the end if you like, following the way her dress curves out. We can even say her sound while we do it, 'lll...'. Lucy Lamp Light says, 'lll...'.

Munching Mike

Objective

To teach the letter shapes and sound for **m** and **M**.

What you need

Letterland materials

- *Big Picture Code Cards*: Munching Mike
- *A-Z Copymasters*: **m** and **Mm**
- *Early Years Handwriting Copymasters*: 13 and 38
- *Early Years Workbook 2*: pages 14-15
- *Letterland Phonics Online*: **Mm**

Other materials

- Tin foil
- Bottle tops
- A variety of different materials such as sand, salt, flour, clay, etc.
- Cereal boxes
- Egg cartons
- Fabric or buttons for eyes
- Button mushrooms
- Marshmallows
- Magnets
- Magnetic objects

Teaching suggestions

Introducing Munching Mike

Show the children the picture of Munching Mike on page 31 of the *Letterland ABC Book* and introduce him using the sample script for **Session 1** (shown right) as a guide for what to say. Invite one or more children to find and touch Munching Mike on the *Letterland Alphabet Frieze*. Ask them to touch his metal head, metal tail, his three metal wheels and his metal mouth.

Munching Mike's letter shape

Introduce **Session 2**. Then sing or chant the handwriting verse shown below (as on the *Handwriting Songs CD* or *Phonics Online*) to help teach Munching Mike's letter shape:

Make Munching Mike's back leg first,
then his second leg, and third,
so he can go munch-munching in a word.

Invite one or more children to finger trace Munching Mike's letter shape on the *ABC Book* or on both sides of the *Big Picture Code Card*.

Munching Mike's sound

To make Munching Mike's sound, ask everyone simply to shut their mouths and hum, and they will be making his sound. Further practice can be found by listening to and singing Mike's song on the *Alphabet Songs CD* or *Letterland Phonics Online*.

Munching Mike's words		
magnet	metal	morning
man	milk	most
mat	miss	mug
me	mix	Mummy
meet	monkey	mushroom
melon	monster	my

Munching Mike sample script

Session 1: Introducing Munching Mike

There's a **m**onster on this page. He's a *lovely* **m**onster. He's a **m**onster that is **m**ade out of **m**etal. If you look, there's something very special about him. He only has *three* legs. Let's count them... one, two three. How unusual! **M**ost creatures have *four* legs or just *two* legs. But not *three* legs like our **m**onster.

Our monster is called **M**unching **M**ike because he loves to munch when he's eating. And you will never believe what **M**unching **M**ike the monster likes to eat best. **M**etal!

You and I would never eat **m**etal. That would

Things to do

- **Munching Mike model** Help to make a model of Munching Mike or a large picture of the metal monster with foil or bottle tops. Make sure he has three legs, not four.
[*KU: Build and construct with a wide range...*]

- **Make marks** Ask the children to pretend to be Munching Mike making his mark (m-shape) in as many different media as practical (e.g. sand, salt, foam, mud, flour, clay etc.).
[*CD: Express and communicate their ideas...*]

- **Monster masks** Help the children to make monster masks. Cut out the backs of cereal boxes and get them to decorate the front and sides. Use paint, egg box parts etc., and fabric or buttons for eyes and ears.
[*KU: Build and construct with a wide range...*]

- **Mushroom pictures** Cut in half some firm button mushrooms. Get the children to press them on to a sponge full of paint and print with them to create 'marvellous mushroom pictures that will make Munching Mike's mouth water'.
[*CD: Explore colour, texture, shape...*]

- **Marshmallows** Hand out some marshmallows to munch as a treat. Then say '**Mmm**...' and rub tummies together. (See *Actions Trick*, page 78.) [*CD: Respond in a variety of ways...*]

- **Further practice** Options for letter shapes:
  - A-Z Copymasters: **m** and **Mm**
  - Early Years Handwriting Copymasters: 13 and 38.
For consolidation of both letter shape and sound use:
  - Early Years Workbook 2, pages 14-15.
  - Letterland Phonics Online.

Things to talk about

- **Menu** Make up a menu for Munching Mike together, not necessarily just food. He eats mops, mats, mugs, metal, magnets, even mushy mud, as well as meat, melons, etc.

- **Magnets** Talk about magnets and let the children see what happens when they put one near paperclips or other magnetic objects.

- **Mistakes** Talk about mistakes. Mike often makes them and gets into muddles, but explain that luckily mistakes often help us to learn.

- **Knowing why** Reminder: see page 19

Explaining the capital M shape

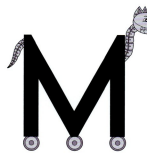

Tell the children that Munching Mike may look big, but he's really only a little monster (too little to start important words). So his Mum does the job of starting important words for him.

---

be far too dangerous! But look, **M**unching **M**ike is **m**unching on a **m**agnet!

If we look at the bottom of the page, we can see some other things that **M**unching **M**ike likes to eat. **M**unching **M**ike is mainly a **m**etal-eating **m**onster. But he also likes to eat **m**ushy things like this **m**elon, or these **m**arshmallows, or that **m**ango. Can you guess what he likes to drink? **Mmmm**! **M**ilk!

Will you be safe when you are with **M**unching **M**ike? Oh, yes! Remember, **M**unching **M**ike likes to eat **m**etal, and you are not made of **m**etal.

Session 2: Munching Mike's shape and sound

I'm sure you'll remember our **m**onster's name. Yes, it's **M**unching **M**ike. Let's count his legs... one, two,

three! That's really unusual, isn't it?

When we **m**ake **M**unching **M**ike's letter, we start by his tail! Are you ready? Let's *start* by his tail, go *down* one leg, back up, *over* to the next leg, back and *over* to his front leg.

Shall we do it again? Let's start by his tail, go *down* his leg, back up *over* to the next leg and down, back *over* to the front leg and down, and stop. Remember, **M**unching **M**ike has one, two, three legs!

Munching **M**ike **m**akes the '**mmm**...' sound. Can you say it with me? Let's say it while we write his letter. Where do we start? By his tail, that's right. Ready? '**Mmm**..., **mmm**...,' and again, '**mmm**..., **mmm**...' for **M**unching **M**ike.

Noisy Nick

Objective

To teach the letter shapes and sound for **n** and **N**.

What you need

Letterland materials

- *Big Picture Code Cards*: Noisy Nick
- *A-Z Copymasters*: **n** and **Nn**
- *Early Years Handwriting Copymasters*: 14 and 39
- *Early Years Workbook 3*: pages 2-3
- *Letterland Phonics Online*: **Nn**

Other materials

- Newspaper
- Sticky tape
- Coloured beads or plastic straws
- String or laces
- Shredded wheat
- Chocolate
- Paper cake cases
- Mini chocolate eggs (if available)
- Assorted nuts, including conkers or acorns (if available)
- Flower seeds

Teaching suggestions

Introducing Noisy Nick

Show the children the picture of Noisy Nick on page 33 of the *ABC Book* and introduce him using the sample script for **Session 1** (shown right) as a guide for what to say. Invite one or more children to find and touch Noisy Nick on the *Alphabet Frieze*. Ask the children also to touch Nick's nose, his nails in **n** and his capital letter shape **N**.

Noisy Nick's letter shape

Introduce **Session 2**. Then sing or chant the handwriting verse shown below (on the *Handwriting Songs CD* or *Letterland Phonics Online*) to help teach Noisy Nick's letter shape:

'Now bang my nail,' Noisy Nick said.
'Go up and over around my head.'

Invite one or more children to finger trace Noisy Nick's letter shape on the *Letterland ABC Book* or on both sides of the *Big Picture Code Card*.

Noisy Nick's sound

Ask the children to press a hand on their nose while they make Nick's '**nnn**...' sound. They will then feel it through the nose as well as hearing it. If they forget his sound, they can just *start* to say Nick's name. Practise Nick's song on the *Alphabet Songs CD* or *Letterland Phonics Online*.

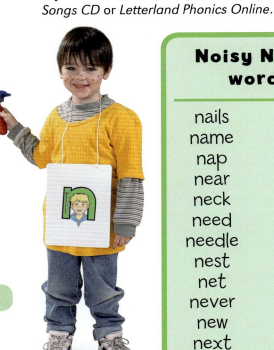

Noisy Nick's words

nails	nice
name	night
nap	nine
near	no
neck	noise
need	nose
needle	not
nest	now
net	number
never	nurse
new	nursery
next	nuts

Noisy Nick sample script

Session 1: Introducing Noisy Nick

I can see a boy on this page. His **n**ame is **N**ick. **N**ow, **N**ick is a **n**ice boy but sometimes he is very **n**oisy, which is **n**ot so **n**ice. In fact, his **n**eighbours have given him a **n**ickname. Do you know what his **n**ickname is? **N**oisy **N**ick! At his home, **N**oisy **N**ick has a hammer and lots of **n**ails. He loves hammering **n**ails but his **n**eighbours don't think it's very **n**ice.

It's **N**oisy **N**ick's **n**inth birthday and he is having a birthday party. He's asked all his Letterland friends over for tea. That cake looks **n**ice! Let's count the candles on the cake. There are **n**ine. What else is there to eat? There's a plate of **n**uts. **N**oisy **N**ick likes **n**uts. Sometimes he picks the

Things to do

- **Necklaces** Let the children make necklaces to wear or give to someone at home. Help them to count out nine beads or nine pieces of chopped up coloured plastic straws, and thread them on to string or laces.
  [PSRN: Talk about, recognise and recreate simple patterns.]

- **Notes** Make little thank-you notes out of card and encourage the children to write 'thank you' on them (or write it for them). Now children can write their names on the notes and think of reasons for giving them to someone.
  [CLL: Attempt writing for various purposes...]

- **Cookery** Make some edible nests. To do this, the children mix shredded wheat into melted chocolate and spoon it into paper cake cases. Add mini chocolate eggs, if available, or cut out little birds from paper folded in half.
  [KU: Look closely at similarities, differences...]

- **Further practice** Options for letter shapes:
  – *A-Z Copymasters:* **n** and **Nn**
  – *Early Years Handwriting Copymasters:* 14 and 39.
  For consolidation of both letter shape and sound use:
  – *Early Years Workbook 3*, pages 2-3.
  – *Letterland Phonics Online*.

Things to talk about

- **Naughty or nice?** Discuss naughty and nice behaviour together. Ask if any of the children can think of a time when they were naughty, and if they felt happy or sad afterwards. Then ask if it makes other people, and themselves, happy when they are nice. Tell them that Noisy Nick is often naughty, but he is slowly learning that being nice is more fun for everyone.

- **Nuts** Provide nuts of different kinds, including conkers or acorns, if available, (but avoiding peanuts) and compare their different sizes and shapes. Compare tree seeds (nuts) with flower seeds, and talk about how one nut can become a big tree that produces hundreds of other nuts. You could then all sing 'I had a little nut tree'.

- **What's new?** Ask if anyone has something new or some new news to share. See if they can notice anything new in the room. You could hang a new number from the ceiling every day.

- **Knowing why** See page 19.

Explaining the capital N shape

Explain to the children that Nick starts important words by using three big nails, which they see in Noisy Nick's name. Tell them that to write his big letter shape, they need to go down the first nail, back up again, down the sloping nail and up the last nail.

---

nuts off his **n**eighbours' **n**ut trees and eats them. Can you see anything in these trees? There's a **n**est in this tree, with eggs in it.

Nick's parents have given him a set of drums for his birthday. Oh **n**o! What will the **n**eighbours say **n**ow? **N**oisy **N**ick will be able to make even more **n**oise than ever!

Goodbye for **n**ow, **N**oisy **N**ick. Try **n**ot to be too **n**oisy before we see you again.

Session 2: Noisy Nick's shape and sound

Do you remember this boy's **n**ame? It's **N**oisy **N**ick. **N**oisy **N**ick has a friend called **N**oisy **N**icola. She is one of his **n**ext door **n**eighbours. When **N**oisy **N**ick and **N**oisy **N**icola are **n**ot hammering **n**ails and making lots of **n**oise,

they like to take their **n**ets and collect **n**uts from all the **n**ut trees in the **n**eighbourhood. Sometimes they see a **n**est in one of the trees. Then they try to be very quiet so they don't disturb any baby birds in the **n**est.

Now look at **N**oisy **N**ick's letter. Can you see a **n**ail in it? To write **N**oisy **N**ick's letter, we **n**eed to start at the top, by the **n**ail, and go *down* the **n**ail and then back round *over* **N**oisy **N**ick's head.

Noisy **N**ick makes the sound at the start of his **n**ame, **Nnn**oisy **Nnn**ick. Can you say, '**nnn**...'? Let's say '**nnn**...' together while we make **N**oisy **N**ick's letter again.

Now you know the '**nnn**...' sound **N**oisy **N**ick makes in words.

Oscar Orange

Objectives

To teach the letter shapes for **o** and **O** and the short vowel sound 'ŏ...', and briefly to introduce the long vowel's name, 'ō...'.

What you need

Letterland materials

- *Big Picture Code Cards*: Oscar Orange and Mr O
- *A-Z Copymasters*: **o** and **Oo**
- *Early Years Handwriting Copymasters*: 15 and 40
- *Early Years Workbook 3*: pages 4-7
- *Letterland Phonics Online*: **Oo**

Other materials

- Orange tissue paper
- Tray
- 6 or 7 small objects
- Toy telephone(s)(if available)
- Any 'office' equipment
- Pipe cleaners or pairs of tights (4 if dense or 8 if thin)
- Needle and thread
- Orange sponge paints
- Oranges

Teaching suggestions

Introducing Oscar Orange

The vowel sounds are the most important sounds for the children to know well, as they occur so often in words. Build in some revision time for all the short vowels learnt so far: the short 'ă...', 'ĕ...' and 'ĭ...' sounds. Then show the children the picture of Oscar Orange on page 35 of the *Letterland ABC Book* and introduce him using the sample script for **Session 1** (shown right) as a guide for what to say. Invite one or more children to find and touch Oscar Orange on the *Letterland Alphabet Frieze*. Ask them to touch him on his nose and on his mouth. Talk briefly about Mr O, the Old Man, too, if asked (see opposite).

Oscar Orange's letter shape

Introduce **Session 2**. Then sing or chant the handwriting verse shown below (on the *Handwriting Songs CD* or *Phonics Online*) to help teach Oscar Orange's letter shape:

> On Oscar Orange start at the top.
> Go all the way round him, and... then stop!

Invite one or more children to finger trace Oscar Orange's letter shape on the *Letterland ABC Book* or on both sides of the *Big Picture Code Card*.

Oscar Orange's sound

Listen and sing Oscar's song on the *Alphabet Songs CD* or *Letterland Phonics Online*. This will help the children to achieve the correct short 'ŏ...' sound.

Oscar Orange's words

object	on
October	olive
octopus	opposite
odd	orange
off	ostrich
office	otter
often	ox

Oscar Orange sample script

Session 1: Introducing Oscar Orange

I can see something I like on this page. That's right. It is a nice round... **o**range, yes! Do you like **o**ranges? Do you eat **o**ranges?

When you eat an **o**range, does all the juice come out? Oh, yes! It sometimes dribbles down your chin, doesn't it? An **o**range is a round juicy fruit. An **o**range rolls away if you're not careful.

But I've never seen an **o**range with such a smily face before, have you? This Letterland **o**range has a special name. His name is **O**scar **O**range. Can you say that for me? **O**scar **O**range. That's right. **O**scar **O**range is a big round **o**range.

Things to do

- **Orange week** Have a special 'orange week' and get everyone to bring in orange objects for an orange collection. Make a feature of a large Oscar Orange, made by the children by sticking crushed orange tissue paper on to a circular outline and then adding arms and a face. Encourage the children to wear something orange, if possible.
  [CLL: Explore and experiment with sounds...]

- **Object game** Play a 'remember the object' game. Place six objects on a tray. While the children close their eyes, put on or take off one object. They look again at the tray and then name the object you put on or took off.
  [PSRN: Use developing mathematical ideas...]

- **Office** Create an office area using toy computers, toy telephones, writing pads, etc. The children can pretend to do office work.
  [CLL: Use language to imagine and recreate roles...]

- **Oscar's octopus** The children can draw or paint an octopus or make one out of pipe cleaners: good practice for counting to eight. Alternatively, stuff four pairs of tights (or eight pairs doubled up) with paper, then tie them together. Use the top of one to make the head and sew it up. Paint the octopus orange using sponge paints and use it for display or play.
  [PSRN: Count reliably up to 10 everyday objects.]

- **Further practice** Options for letter shapes:
  – *Lower Case Pictogram Copymasters:* **o** and **Oo**
  – *Early Years Handwriting Copymasters:* 15 and 40.
  For consolidation of both letter shape and sound use:
  – *Early Years Workbook 3*, pages 4-7.
  – *Letterland Phonics Online*.

Things to talk about

- **Oranges** Bring in a few oranges to talk about. Ask the children if they know where they come from and what the weather is like where they grow, what they grow on, what colour they are and why they have pips (seeds) inside. Ask if any children like oranges or orange juice.

- **Opposites** Talk about the meaning of the word **opposite**. Discuss opposites such as on and off, day and night, hot and cold, etc.

Explaining the capital O shape

Tell the children that when Oscar Orange is needed to start an important word, he takes a deep breath and gets bigger. Then he gets on with making his 'ŏ...' sound as usual.

Introducing Mr O, the Old Man

Introduce Mr O, the Old Man, using either the *Alphabet Frieze* or the *Big Picture Code Cards*. Explain that Mr O brings oranges to Letterland from over the ocean by boat. Nobody knows how old he is, but they do know he is old, because of his white beard. At special times Mr O goes into words and says his name, 'ō...', as in **old**.

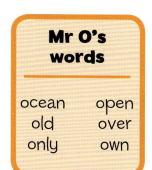

Mr O's words

ocean	open
old	over
only	own

Is his letter shape round too? Yes, it is! Let's say his name again, **O**scar **O**range.

That's a very **o**dd creature in the sea, as well. It's an **o**ctopus. An **o**ctopus has eight legs. How many **o**ranges is our **o**ctopus playing with? Yes, he's playing with three **o**ranges. Hello, **o**ctopus!

It's time to wave goodbye to **O**scar **O**range. We'll visit him again another day.

Session 2: Oscar Orange's shape and sound

Here's our **o**range with a smily face again. Can you remember his name? Yes, he's called **O**scar **O**range. Look at his round shape. His letter shape is round too, isn't it!

When we want to write **O**scar's letter, we start over here by his leaf, we go over the top of his head, all the way round under **O**scar **O**range and back up again. Are you ready? Start at his leaf. Go over the top of his head, all the way round **O**scar **O**range and back up again.

Can you hear the sound at the beginning of **O**scar's name: 'ŏ..., ŏ..., ŏ...'? Did you know when you say his sound, your mouth makes a round shape, like his letter? You look at my mouth and I'll look at your mouth. Shall we say it together? 'Ŏ... ŏ...'. Did my mouth look as round as **O**scar? Your mouth did as well! 'Ŏ..., ŏ...' for Ŏscar Ŏrange.

Peter Puppy

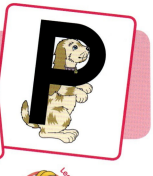

Objective

To teach the letter shapes and sound for **p** and **P**.

What you need

Letterland materials

- *Big Picture Code Cards*: Peter Puppy
- *A-Z Copymasters*: **p** and **Pp**
- *Early Years Handwriting Copymasters*: 16 and 41
- *Early Years Workbook 3*: pages 8-9
- *Letterland Phonics Online*: **Pp**

Other materials

- Pattern-making or mosaic peg boards
- Potatoes and other foods beginning with **p**
- Pink and purple paint
- Dried pasta (in a variety of shapes)
- Prize for 'Pass the parcel'
- Paper bags

Teaching suggestions

Introducing Peter Puppy

Show the children the picture of Peter Puppy on page 37 of the *ABC Book* and introduce him using the sample script for **Session 1** (shown right) as a guide for what to say. Invite one or more children to find and touch Peter Puppy on the *Alphabet Frieze*. Ask them to point to his droopy ear, his purple collar, his paws and pale brown patches.

Peter Puppy's letter shape

Introduce **Session 2**. Sing/chant the hand-writing verse shown below (*Handwriting Songs CD* or *Phonics Online*) to help teach Peter Puppy's shape:

Pat Peter Puppy properly.
First stroke down his ear,
then up and round his face
so he won't shed a tear.

Invite one or more children to finger trace Peter Puppy's letter shape on the *Letterland ABC Book* or on both sides of the *Big Picture Code Card*.

Peter Puppy's sound

This is one of the sounds which needs to be whispered to avoid adding 'uh'. The sound is simply a puff of air pushed through closed lips. Let the children imagine they are panting like a puppy, while making the '**p**...' sound. Listening to Peter Puppy's song on the *Alphabet Songs CD* or on *Phonics Online* software will also help them to achieve the correct sound.

Peter Puppy's words

paint	pencil	pony
paper	pet	present
parcel	picture	pretty
park	pig	puddle
party	pink	pull
pass	play	puppy
paw	please	purple
pen	pond	put

Peter Puppy sample script

Session 1: Introducing Peter Puppy

There's a **p**uppy on this **p**age. He's **p**laying in the Letterland **p**ark with his **p**als. His name is **P**eter **P**uppy.

Peter **P**uppy looks very happy here, but sometimes he is very sad. Do you know why he is sometimes sad? Let me tell you. He has long droopy ears and he can't make those ears **p**rick up. They always droop down. **P**oor **p**uppy, he would love to have ears that **p**oint up like a **p**olice dog's ears! But never mind, he seems **p**erfectly happy today!

Maybe it's because he has a **p**resent to open. Can you **p**oint to it in the **p**icture? **P**erhaps the

Things to do

- **Patterns** The children can experiment with making patterns on paper by repeating different lines or shapes, for instance, by drawing round a couple of objects and then repeating the sequence to make a pattern. They could also play with any pattern-making boards or mosaic peg boards.
  [PSRN: Talk about, recognise and recreate...]

- **Potato printing** Do some potato printing with the children. Cut potatoes into a variety of shapes, including petal shapes and paw shapes. Make prints using pink and purple paint.
  [PSRN: Talk about, recognise and recreate...]

- **'Pass the parcel'** Play 'Pass the parcel', Peter Puppy's favourite game.
  [PSE: Maintain attention, concentrate and sit...]

- **Peter Puppy puppets** Help the children to make Peter Puppy puppets, or other puppets of their favourite Letterland characters. Cut out photocopies of the desired characters from the *A-Z Copymasters* or the *Early Years Handwriting Copymasters* and paste them on to paper bags. The children can then colour them in or paint them. Try having a little puppet show with them.
  [CLL: Use language to imagine and recreate...]

- **People pictures** Ask the children to draw pictures of people. Encourage them to look for details, and not to forget features such as the nose, ears, hands or feet.
  [KU: Find out about and identify some features...]

- **Peter Puppy's foods** Possibilities for snacks include popcorn, pretzels, peaches, pears, pancakes.
  [CD: Respond in a variety of ways...]

- **Further practice** Options for letter shapes:
  – *A-Z Copymasters:* **p** and **Pp**
  – *Early Years Handwriting Copymasters:* 16 and 41.
  For consolidation of both letter shape and sound use:
  – *Early Years Workbook 3*, pages 8-9.
  – *Letterland Phonics Online.*

Things to talk about

- **Politeness** Tell the children that Peter Puppy always says, 'Please stroke me properly.' Ask them if they say 'please' often enough, and suggest that they let Peter Puppy help them to remember to say it whenever needed, especially this week.

- **Making plans** Talk about making plans. Perhaps the children could help to plan a party and make or wrap up little prizes for party games.

- **Parents** Help everyone to think of ways that they can give some pleasure to their parents.

Explaining the capital P shape

Explain that when Peter Puppy has a chance to start an important word, he is so pleased, that he pops up so that everyone can see him better. He hopes his ears will pop up too, but sadly they still droop.

---

penguins gave it to him! How many **p**enguins can you see? One, two, three. Is this another **p**enguin in the **p**alm tree? No, it's a bird called a **p**igeon. And what is this **p**retty bird called, next to the **p**inecones? It's a **p**arrot.

Session 2: Peter Puppy's shape and sound

Can you remember this **p**uppy's name? Yes, it's **P**eter **P**uppy. Do you think he would like you to gently stroke his **p**oor droopy ears? He loves to have you stroke his ear when you write his letter. Shall I show you how he likes to be stroked? We start at the top of his droopy ear, we go *down*, *up* and *round* his face to finish under his chin. Let's try it right now!

Start at the top of his droopy ear, go *down*, *up* and *round* his face to finish under his chin. Let's make **P**eter **P**uppy's sound too. It's a little panting sound, like when a puppy is out of breath, '**p**..., **p**..., **p**...'. You try it, '**p**..., **p**..., **p**...'. while I stroke his ear.

He loves it if we always stroke down his droopy ear first. Do you remember why he is sometimes sad? It's because he can't make his ears **p**oint up! Sometimes he even cries. Do you know what sound his tears make when they fall into a **p**uddle? **P**lip, **p**lop. **P**lip, **p**lop.

Those words, **plip**, **plop**, start with **P**eter **P**uppy's sound, don't they? '**P**...' for **p**lip and '**p**...' for **p**lop! That's **P**eter **P**uppy's sound.

Quarrelsome Queen

Objective

To teach the letter shapes and sound for **q** and **Q**.

What you need

Letterland materials

- *Big Picture Code Cards*: Quarrelsome Queen
- *A-Z Copymasters*: **q** and **Qq**
- *Early Years Handwriting Copymasters*: 17 and 41
- *Early Years Workbook 3*: pages 10-11
- *Letterland Phonics Online*: **Qq**

Other materials

- Card or paper for crowns (gold if available)
- Coloured paper (preferably gummed) or tin foil
- Paper squares
- Old magazines or other patterned paper

Teaching suggestions

Introducing Quarrelsome Queen

Show the children the picture of Quarrelsome Queen on page 39 of the *ABC Book* and introduce her using the sample script for **Session 1** (shown right) as a guide for what to say. Invite one or more children to find and touch Quarrelsome Queen on the *Alphabet Frieze*. Ask them to point to her crown and her beautiful long hair.

Quarrelsome Queen's letter shape

Introduce **Session 2**. Then sing or chant the handwriting verse shown below (as on the *Handwriting Songs CD* or *Phonics Online*) to help teach Quarrelsome Queen's letter shape:

Quickly go round the Queen's cross face.
Then comb her beautiful hair into place.

Invite one or more children to finger trace Quarrelsome Queen's letter shape on the *ABC Book* or on both sides of the *Big Picture Code Card*.

Quarrelsome Queen's sound

Quarrelsome Queen's sound is really two others put together: '**kw**...'.
The queen's song on the *Alphabet Songs CD* or *Letterland Phonics Online* will help in achieving the correct sound.

Quarrelsome Queen's words

quack
quarrelsome
quarter
queen
question
queue
quick
quiet
quill
quilt
quite
quiz

Quarrelsome Queen sample script

Session 1: Introducing Quarrelsome Queen

Oh, dear. Did you know there's a **q**ueen in Letterland? How do I know she's a **q**ueen? That's right. She always has a crown on her head. But I'd better tell you this **q**uietly. She's a very **q**uarrelsome **q**ueen.

Do you ever **q**uarrel? Yes, I **q**uarrel sometimes. When I **q**uarrel, I feel as cross as that **q**ueen looks. **Q**uarrelling makes me feel sad. Does it make you feel sad? Soon after I've **q**uarrelled I have to go back and say, 'I'm sorry.' That makes me feel better again.

When this **q**uarrelsome **q**ueen **q**uarrels, she feels sad afterwards, too. She tells herself she'll

Things to do

- **Queen's crown** Prepare strips of gold or yellow card or paper to make into Quarrelsome Queen's crowns. If neither is available, use white card coloured in by the children. Decorate with gummed coloured paper or tin foil. Then staple each crown to fit the children.
  [CD: Use their imagination in art and design...]

- **Queuing game** Tell the children to make a queue and to move quietly. Direct them to move the queue forwards, or to one side, or around a chair. Talk to the children about why we need to form queues.
  [PSRN: Work as part of a group or class...]

- **Queuing picture** On a large piece of paper, draw or paint the Queen on the far right, and then let the children draw or paint pictures of themselves in a queue to see her.
  [PSRN: Use everyday words to describe position.]

- **Queen's quilt collage** Make a Queen's quilt collage together by pasting coloured or patterned paper (from magazines, etc.) onto a large sheet of paper. The Queen's face can then be drawn in at the top of it. Don't let the children forget to add her umbrella, too!
  [CD: Use their imagination in art, design...]

- **Further practice** Options for letter shapes:
  – *A-Z Copymasters:* **q** and **Qq**
  – *Early Years Handwriting Copymasters:* 17 and 41.
  For consolidation of both letter shape and sound use:
  – *Early Years Workbook 3*, pages 10-11.
  – *Letterland Phonics Online.*

Things to talk about

- **Queen's umbrella** The script below points out that Quarrelsome Queen never goes anywhere without her umbrella, because **q** never appears in words without **u**. Two children can act this out in front of the others. One child can be dressed up as the Queen, and another one can hold up a real umbrella and follow her around the room. This will also help to avoid confusion between the **p** and **q** letter shapes.

- **Quarrelsome Queen's quarrelling** Invite the children to suggest why Quarrelsome Queen quarrels with some of the Letterland characters. Maybe it is because Noisy Nick makes too much noise banging nails or perhaps Red Robot took her ruby ring?

- **Being quiet** Talk about being quiet. See who can say their name using the quietest voice. Let the children take it in turns to try. Then see who can walk with quiet steps and who can stand up and sit down so quietly that you cannot hear them.

- **Being quick** Tell the children that the Queen often says, 'Quick, quick!' See how quickly they can tidy up today.

Explaining the capital Q shape

This very different capital letter shape is the 'Queen's Quiet room'. It has nothing in it except a place for her to sit very quietly.

---

stop, but before she knows it, she's **q**uarrelling again. She's always **q**uarrelling. That's why we call her **Q**uarrelsome **Q**ueen.

And do you know something else that's special about the Letterland **q**ueen? She never goes anywhere without her umbrella. Do you see it there beside her, on top of the **q**uilt? **Q**uarrelsome **Q**ueen *always* has her umbrella with her when she goes into words.

Session 2: Quarrelsome Queen's shape and sound

If you look closely at this **q**ueen's face you'll easily remember her name. Yes, it's **Q**uarrelsome **Q**ueen.

Can you remember what **Q**uarrelsome **Q**ueen

takes with her wherever she goes? Yes, she always takes her umbrella with her. **Q**uarrelsome **Q**ueen says 'kw...' for **q**uarrel, 'kw...' for **q**ueen. It's a very **q**uiet sound.

Shall we make her letter? We start off by the back of her crown, we go *all* the way round her face, *up* to her crown and *down* her long hair. Let's try again. We start by her crown, go *round* her face, *up* to her crown and *down* her long hair. And let's make her **q**uiet sound together. 'Kw..., kw...' for **Q**uarrelsome **Q**ueen.

The **Q**ueen has a big round **Q**uiet Room that she goes into after she's been **q**uarrelling. But she even takes her umbrella there. Be **q**uiet, now. We don't want to disturb **Q**uarrelsome **Q**ueen.

Red Robot

Objective

To teach the letter shapes and sound for **r** and **R**.

What you need

Letterland materials

- *Big Picture Code Cards*: Red Robot
- *A-Z Copymasters*: **r** and **Rr**
- *Early Years Handwriting Copymasters*: 18 and 42
- *Early Years Workbook 3*: pages 12-13
- *Letterland Phonics Online*: **Rr**

Other materials

- Large tray or smooth board
- Variety of small objects, some that roll
- Several shades of red paper

Teaching suggestions

Introducing Red Robot

Show the children the picture of Red Robot on page 41 of the *Letterland ABC Book* and introduce him using the sample script for **Session 1** (shown right) as a guide for what to say. Invite one or more children to find and touch Red Robot on the *Letterland Alphabet Frieze*. Ask them to touch his red head and legs, and his red and silver roller-skates. Talk about the capital **R** pictogram if asked (see opposite).

Red Robot's letter shape

Introduce **Session 2**. Then sing or chant the handwriting verse shown below (as on the *Handwriting Songs CD* or *Phonics Online*) to help teach Red Robot's letter shape:

Run down Red Robot's body.
Go up to his arm and his hand.
Then watch out for this robot
roaming round Letterland.

Invite one or more children to finger trace Red Robot's letter shape on the *ABC Book* or on both sides of the *Big Picture Code Card*.

Red Robot's sound

Children will need to avoid adding an unwanted 'uh' sound by keeping their teeth touching while making Red Robot's growling sound. They must not move their chins as they 'growl'. Red Robot's song on the *Alphabet Songs CD* or *Letterland Phonics Online* will help in achieving the correct sound.

Red Robot's words

rabbit	red	roof
race	ride	rope
radio	right	roses
rain	ring	round
rascal	road	rubber
rat	robber	ruler
read	robot	rules
ready	rock	run
really	roll	rush

Red Robot sample script

Session 1: Introducing Red Robot

Now here's **R**ed **R**obot. **R**ed **R**obot is a **r**eal **r**ascal. He takes things that don't belong to him. We don't like that, do we!

Can you see what he has in his hand? Yes! He has a **r**emote-control. He has a **r**ed **r**emote-control for his **r**ed **r**acing car.

Ah! Look at the things in his sack. He has taken someone's **r**oller skates. He has taken somebody's **r**adio as well. And I think I can see a big **r**ed **r**uler in his sack.

Red **R**obot **r**uns very quickly. Why do you think he **r**uns? Yes! So that people can't catch him and see all the things that he has taken.

Things to do

- **Red collection** Let the children paint a large picture of Red Robot and display red objects beside it. Encourage the children to wear something red, if possible.
[CD: Explore colour, texture, shape...]

- **Rolling** Make a slight slope using a tray or smooth board for rolling various small objects down. Ask the children to guess which objects will roll. (Sliding does not count.)
[KU: Ask questions about why things happen...]

- **Road safety** Use a road mat, toy cars and toy people for play and for teaching basic road safety.
[KU: Find out about, and identify features...]

- **Red pictures** Provide different shades of red paper and any other materials for the children to make a variety of red collage pictures. Display them with your red collection (see above).
[CD: Explore colour, texture, shape...]

- **Robots** Help the children to construct robots out of junk.
[CD: Use their imagination in art and design...]

- **Red Robot's rainbow** Talk about the colours of the rainbow and ask children to paint one.
[CD: Explore colour, texture, shape...]

- **Further practice** Options for letter shapes:
  – *A-Z Copymasters:* **r** and **Rr**
  – *Early Years Handwriting Copymasters:* 18 and 42.
For consolidation of both letter shape and sound use:
  – *Early Years Workbook 3*, pages 12-13.
  – *Letterland Phonics Online.*

Things to talk about

- **Robbing** Think of some things that the rascal Red Robot would take because they start with his sound.

- **Favourite foods** Ask if Red Robot would prefer his potatoes baked or roasted, and then let the children suggest some more of his favourite foods, such as **raspberries**, **rolls**, **rice**, **radishes**, **red jelly**, **raisins**, etc.

- **Favourite pastimes** Help the children to decide what Red Robot would most enjoy doing. Perhaps he would ride round and round in a racing car or roller skate by the river.

- **Rule breaker** Explain that Red Robot is a rule breaker who takes other people's things. Stress that it's not right and that we don't want to be like him!

- **Tongue twister** Try saying together the tongue twister 'Round and round the rugged rock the ragged rascal (or perhaps, real rascal) ran.'

Explaining the capital R shape

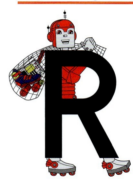

Tell the children that when he starts somebody's name, Red Robot takes a big breath and gets bigger. He even changes his letter shape to make it harder for us to recognise him. So don't be fooled by this red rascal!

Red **R**obot is a **r**ascal in Letterland. He's always in **r**eal trouble, so he's always **r**unning away.

Can you make your fingers **r**un like **R**ed **R**obot's two legs? Change your two fingers into two legs. That's **r**ight.

Are you **rrr**eady with your fingers to **r**un fast? Make them **r**un. And again. **R**un, **r**un, **r**un away like **R**ed **R**obot.

Session 2: Red Robot's shape and sound

I'm sure you can **r**emember this **r**ascal's name. Yes, it's **R**ed **R**obot. Can you **r**emember some of the things **R**ed **R**obot has taken? Yes, some **r**oller skates and a **r**adio.

Let's see *you* use your fingers to make **r**unning

legs and **r**un your fingers along like **R**ed **R**obot.

When **R**ed **R**obot **r**olls into words, he makes a growling sound, like this: '**rrr**..., **rrr**..., **rrr**...' *(through closed teeth)*. Let's make his sound together, '**rrr**..., **rrr**..., **rrr**...'. Can you hear that growling sound at the beginning of his name, **Rrr**ed **Rrr**obot? That's the sound he makes in words like **rrr**un and **rrr**ed and **rrr**uler and **rrr**adio... yes, and **rrr**oller skates.

When we make **R**ed **R**obot's letter, we start at his neck. We go *down* to his leg, back up and *round* that arm. Are you **r**eady? We start at his neck, go *down* to his leg, back up and *round* his arm, and we say the sound, '**rrr**..., **rrr**...', again, '**rrr**..., **rrr**...' for **R**ed **R**obot.

Sammy Snake

Objective

To teach the letter shapes and sound for **s** and **S**.

What you need

Letterland materials

- *Big Picture Code Cards*: Sammy Snake
- *A-Z Copymasters*: **s** and **Ss**
- *Early Years Handwriting Copymasters*: 19 and 43
- *Early Years Workbook 3*: pages 14-15
- *Letterland Phonics Online*: **Ss**

Other materials

- Stocking
- Newspaper
- Needle and thread
- Sponge pads
- Green and yellow paint
- Pipe cleaners
- Pairs of socks
- Washing line or string
- Pegs

Teaching suggestions

Introducing Sammy Snake

Show the children the picture of Sammy Snake on page 43 of the *Letterland ABC Book* and introduce him using the sample script for **Session 1** (shown right) as a guide for what to say. Invite one or more children to find and touch Sammy Snake on the *Alphabet Frieze*. Ask them to touch his head and his yellow and green striped tail.

Sammy Snake's letter shape

Introduce **Session 2**. Then sing or chant the handwriting verse shown below (as on the *Handwriting Songs CD* or *Phonics Online*) to help teach Sammy Snake's letter shape:

**Start at Sam's head where he can see.
Stroke down to his tail, oh so care-ful-ly!**

Invite one or more children to finger trace Sammy Snake's letter shape on the *Letterland ABC Book* or on both sides of the *Big Picture Code Card*.

Sammy Snake's sound

This is a simple hissing sound. If a child adds voice instead of whispering it, the result will be 'sssuh', so stress the hiss as a whispered sound. Sammy Snake's song on the *Alphabet Songs CD* or *Letterland Phonics Online* will help in achieving the correct sound.

Sammy Snake's words

sad	snail
sand	snake
sandals	soap
sausages	socks
school	sound
scissors	soup
seaside	special
seesaw	spider
sister	star
six	start
sky	summer
sleep	sun
small	sweets

Sammy Snake sample script

Session 1: Introducing Sammy Snake

This time, before I open my book, you have to be *very* quiet because we're going to meet **s**omebody very **s**pecial. This creature makes a **s**pecial hissing **s**ound. Are you ready? Be very quiet so you can hear. I'm opening the book carefully and I'm making his sound, '**sss**...'

Did you hear it? Can *you* make it for me? That's right. And who is it making that **s**ound? A **s**nake. Oh, but look at that **s**miling **s**nake. Do you think you need to be frightened of this **s**nake? No, I don't. That's because he's a friendly Letterland **s**nake. Would you like to know what this **s**nake is

Things to do

- **Sleeping snakes** Ask the children to pretend to be snakes. They can all lie down on their stomachs and slither and slide like Sammy Snake. Then they can pretend to sleep. Choose two children to stand up and take small steps around the sleeping snakes.
  [PD: Move with control and co-ordinate...]

- **Sandpit** Suggest that the children draw Sammy Snake's letter in the sand six or seven times and count them.
  [CLL: Attempt writing for various purposes...]

- **Stocking Sammy** Help the children to stuff stockings with crumpled newspaper. Sew or tie up the ends for them. Children can now decorate their snakes using sponge pads of green and yellow paint to make stripes.
  [CD: Explore colour, texture, shape...]

- **Pipe cleaner Sammy** Ask the children to bend pipe cleaners into s-shapes and mount them on to paper using glue. Explain that the snakes should be mounted looking in the Reading Direction. Draw faces and tails.
  [CLL: Link sounds to letters...]

- **Sorting socks** Bring in some pairs of socks. Get the children to sort them into matching pairs, then display them on 'Sammy Snake's sock line' with pegs.
  [PSRN: Use developing mathematical ideas...]

- **Further practice** Options for letter shapes:
  – *A-Z Copymasters:* s and **Ss**
  – *Early Years Handwriting Copymasters*: 19 and 43.
For consolidation of both letter shape and sound use:
  – *Early Years Workbook 3*, pages 14-15.
  – *Letterland Phonics Online*.

Things to talk about

- **Socks** Following on from the sock sorting activity, find out which is the smallest sock, the longest and the widest sock. Ask what kind of socks the children like best and what kind they think Sammy Snake might have, perhaps striped socks. Let them decide how many he would need: one or none?

- **Seaside** Talk about what Sammy Snake might like beginning with his sound at the seaside. Also talk about anything the children themselves enjoy.

- **Sun** Talk about how the sun helps to keep us warm, and makes the flowers grow and open. Warn about the dangers of too much sun.

- **Sausages** Learn the counting rhyme 'Ten fat sausages sizzling in the pan'.

- **Favourite foods** Ask what the children think Sammy Snake might like for a snack. He likes anything starting with his sound, for example, **soup**, **sandwiches**, **sausage rolls**, **sweets**, **spaghetti**, **strawberries**, **spiders**, even when they are all **sandy**!

Explaining the capital S shape

Explain that whenever Sammy Snake has a chance to start an important word, like a name or a word on a sign, he takes a deep breath and gets bigger. Then people call him a 'super-size snake'.

---

called? He's **S**ammy **S**nake.

Where is **S**ammy **S**nake? Yes, he's at the Letterland **s**wimming pool, right next to the **s**ea. Look, he's **s**itting in the **s**un with **s**ome of his friends. They look like they're having a really **sss**uper time!

Session 2: Sammy Snake's shape and sound

Do you remember our **s**wimming pool picture? Who do we **s**ee having a **s**uper time in the **s**un at the **s**ide of the **s**wimming pool? Yes, it's **S**ammy **S**nake. Do you remember the **s**ound he makes at the beginning of his name? **S**ay it with me, '**S**ammy **S**nake **s**ays '**sss**...'.'

Do you hear his **s**pecial **s**ound at the beginning

of **sss**un? And what's that beside **S**ammy **S**nake? Yes, it's a **s**andwich. Does the word **s**andwich **s**tart with **S**ammy's **s**pecial **s**ound? Listen, **sss**andwich. And **sss**unglasses **s**tarts with a hiss, too.

What is that thing with a yellow and blue **s**ail? A **s**ailboat. Does the word **sss**ailboat **s**tart with **S**ammy **S**nake's **s**pecial **s**ound? Yes, it does. Oh, **S**ammy **S**nake loves being by the **s**wimming pool, eating **s**andwiches in the **s**un.

Let's **s**ay his **s**ound while we make his letter. We're going to **s**tart by his head, go *all* the way *round* his body and *down* to his tail. Ready?

Start by his head, go *round* his body and *down* to his tail and let's **s**ay '**sss**...' together. That's **S**ammy **S**nake at the **s**wimming pool.

Talking Tess

Objective

To teach the letter shapes and sound for **t** and **T**.

What you need

Letterland materials

- *Big Picture Code Cards*: Talking Tess
- *A-Z Copymasters*: **t** and **Tt**
- *Early Years Handwriting Copymasters*: 20 and 44
- *Early Years Workbook 4*: pages 2-3
- *Letterland Phonics Online*: **Tt**

Other materials

- Long cardboard tubes
- Coloured cellophane
- Teddy shapes
- Small paper circles or buttons
- Buttons
- Shoe or egg boxes
- Toy train set
- Bread for making toast or mini toasts
- Toy telephone
- Clock face

Teaching suggestions

Introducing Talking Tess

Show the children the picture of Talking Tess on page 45 of the *ABC Book* and introduce her using the sample script for **Session 1** (shown right) as a guide. Invite one or more children to find and touch Talking Tess on the *Alphabet Frieze*. Ask them to touch her head, toes and telephone.

Talking Tess's letter shape

Introduce **Session 2**. Then sing or chant the handwriting verse shown below (as on the *Handwriting Songs CD* or *Letterland Phonics Online*) to help teach Talking Tess's shape:

Tall as a tower make Talking Tess stand.
Go from head to toe,
and then from hand to hand.

Invite one or more children to finger trace Talking Tess's letter shape on the *Letterland ABC Book* or on both sides of the *Big Picture Code Card*.

Talking Tess's sound

The children need to avoid saying 'tuh' by whispering this sound. To help them, ask them to touch the top of their mouths with their tongues.

Then they can just *start* to say, 'Talking Tess'. Talking Tess's song on the *Alphabet Songs CD* or *Letterland Phonics Online* will help them to achieve the correct sound.

Talking Tess's words

table	tiny
tall	top
tap	toy
tea	tractor
teddy	train
telephone	tree
telescope	trousers
tell	true
ten	turn
tent	twice

Talking Tess sample script

Session 1: Introducing Talking Tess

It's **t**ime for us to say hello to **T**alking **T**ess! We have to catch her when she's not **t**oo busy **t**alking on the **t**elephone. She works in the **T**eletouch **T**ower block and her job is keeping everyone in Letterland in **t**ouch with each other. That means she's often **t**alking on the **t**elephone all day long. No wonder everyone calls her 'Talking **T**ess'!

Can you see a **t**iny **t**elephone in **T**alking **T**ess's hand? It's called a mobile phone. She **t**akes it with her everywhere she goes so she won't miss any phone calls.

In her office **T**alking **T**ess is in charge of all the **t**elephones and **t**elevision sets in Letterland.

Things to do

- **Building towers** Suggest that the children build some tall towers with building bricks. How tall can they make the tower before it tips and topples over?
  [KU: Build and construct with a wide range...]

- **Tess's telescope** Make telescopes for Talking Tess with long cardboard tubes from tin foil or kitchen roll. Let the children paint them, or cover them with coloured paper. Fix coloured cellophane (e.g. from sweet wrappers) over the ends with elastic bands, and then see how the world looks!
  [KU: Ask questions about why things happen...]

- **Teddy pictures** Prepare some teddy shapes and provide assorted small circles of paper or buttons. The children can stick on two circles for eyes, one circle for a nose and three buttons down teddy's tum, then draw his mouth.
  [PSRN: Say and use number names in order...]

- **Treasure chest** The children can paint then decorate a small box with a lid (for example, a child's shoe box or an egg box) to be a 'treasure chest' for tiny toys.
  [CD: Express and communicate their ideas...]

- **Trains, tracks and tunnels** Using model train sets, let the children build trains, tracks and tunnels. Talk about travelling by train, like Tess.
  [KU: Ask questions about why things happen...]

- **Tea party** Have a tea party or a teddy bear's picnic. Drink pretend tea and serve tiny pieces of real toast. (Talking Tess loves tea and toast.)
  [PSE: Form good relationships with adults and...]

- **Further practice** Options for letter shapes:
  – *A-Z Copymasters:* **t** and **Tt**
  – *Early Years Handwriting Copymasters:* 20 and 44.
  For consolidation of both letter shape and sound use:
  – *Early Years Workbook 4*, pages 2-3.
  – *Letterland Phonics Online*.

Things to talk about

- **Talking to Tess** Hand a toy mobile phone around for the children to talk to Tess. Another child (or you) can be Tess. Suggest that they ask Tess what time it is in Letterland, invite her to tea, or simply chat with her.

- **Counting to ten** Practise counting to ten with the children, or even to twenty. Tell them that Talking Tess thinks that's terrific. Use terrific as your main word of praise during this week.

- **Toys** Ask each child to tell everyone about a favourite toy, or to talk about a toy that he or she would like to be given.

- **Knowing why** Reminder: see page 19.

Explaining the capital T shape

Tell the children that when Talking Tess starts her name (or another), she takes a deep breath and grows so tall that her head disappears in the clouds. We still know it's Tess, however, because we can still see her arms.

She knows how to fix them, too, when they stop working. Can you see the **t**rain behind her? Every morning **T**alking **T**ess travels by **t**rain to get to work at the **T**eletouch **T**ower block.

Look closely now. Can you find a **t**eddy bear in the picture? Did you know **T**alking **T**ess loves **t**eddy bears? Perhaps it's because the word **t**eddy begins with her **t**iny 't...' sound: **t**..., **t**..., **t**... teddy. It's at the start of **T**alking **T**ess's name too. **t**..., **t**..., **t**...**T**alking **T**ess. Let's all whisper it together.

Session 2: Talking Tess's shape and sound

Do you remember this **t**all person's name? It's **T**alking **T**ess. She works in the Teletouch Tower block, doesn't she? Her name starts with a tiny '**t**...' sound. Listen, **T**alking **T**ess, **t**..., **t**..., **t**.... And so does the word **t**elephone, **t**..., **t**..., **t**... telephone.

Talking **T**ess has a **t**all letter shape. When we write her letter, we start at her neck, go *all* the way down to her **t**oes, and then we make her arms. Ready? Start at her neck, go *all* the way down to her **t**oes and then make her arms.

While we do it this **t**ime, let's say, '**t**..., **t**..., **t**...'. We're going to start by her neck, go down to her **t**oes, and then go across to her **t**elephone hand. And we're going to say, '**t**..., **t**..., **t**...' because this is the sound that **T**alking **T**ess makes in words.

Uppy Umbrella

Objectives

To teach the letter shapes for **u** and **U** and the short vowel sound 'ŭ...', and briefly to introduce the long vowel's name, 'ū...'.

What you need

Letterland materials

- *Big Picture Code Cards*: Uppy Umbrella and Mr U
- *A-Z Copymasters*: **u** and **Uu**
- *Early Years Handwriting Copymasters*: 21 and 45
- *Early Years Workbook 4*: pages 4-5
- *Letterland Phonics Online*: **Uu**

Other materials

- Paper cups
- Sweets (for each child)

Teaching suggestions

Introducing Uppy Umbrella

Before introducing the short 'ŭ...' sound, it is a good idea to revise the short 'ă...', 'ĕ...', 'ĭ...' and 'ŏ...' sounds. Then show the children the picture of Uppy Umbrella on page 47 of the *Letterland ABC Book* and introduce him using the sample script for **Session 1** (shown right) as a guide for what to say. Invite one or more children to find and touch Uppy Umbrella on the *Letterland Alphabet Frieze*. Talk briefly about the capital **U** and about Mr U in his uniform, if asked (see opposite).

Uppy Umbrella's letter shape

Introduce **Session 2**. Then sing or chant the handwriting verse shown below (as on the *Handwriting Songs CD* or *Letterland Living ABC*) to help teach Uppy Umbrella's letter shape:

Under the umbrella draw a shape like a cup.
Then draw a straight line so it won't tip up.

Invite one or more children to finger trace Uppy Umbrella's letter shape on both sides of the *Big Picture Code Card*.

Uppy Umbrella's sound

Just ask the children to start to say Uppy's name to make her sound. For once there is no 'uh' sound to avoid, because 'uh' *is* her sound. Uppy Umbrella's song on the *Alphabet Songs CD* or on the *Letterland Phonics Online* will help in achieving the correct sound.

Uppy Umbrella's words

ugly	underneath	unusual
umbrella	understand	up
unbutton	undone	upside down
uncle	unhappy	upstairs
under	unless	us

Uppy Umbrella sample script

Session 1: Introducing Uppy Umbrella

I want you to close your eyes before I open my book. Close your eyes very tightly, and very carefully open your hands. I want you to pretend that it's raining. If it's raining, what would you feel on your hands? That's right. You would feel the raindrops. Lift your hands **u**p a little, **u**p, **u**p, **u**p. Can you feel the rain as you pretend that rain is falling on to your fingers? Lift them again. **U**p, **u**p, **u**p. That's right.

You can open your eyes now. When it really rains, I don't put my hands **u**p. I put something else **u**p. Can you tell me what else I put **u**p? Perhaps if you look at my picture it will help? Yes, I put **up** an **u**mbrella.

Why do I put **up** an **u**mbrella? To keep me

Things to do

- **Upside down** The observation game 'Upside down' is brief, but fun to play often, especially during your Uppy Umbrella week. From time to time, secretly turn something in the room upside down. Ask the children, 'What's unusual now?' and let them reply, 'The book (picture, teddy bear, etc.) is upside down.'
[PSRN: Use everyday words to describe position.]

- **Under the cup** Lay out the same number of paper cups as there are children, placing the cups upside down. Hide one sweet under a cup and ask the children in turn to lift up a cup. The winner gets the sweet, then sits out while the others cover up their eyes and you hide the next sweet. Repeat until everybody has a sweet.
[CLL: Interact with others, negotiating plans...]

- **Further practice** Options for letter shapes:
  – *A-Z Copymasters:* **u** and **Uu**
  – *Early Years Handwriting Copymasters:* 21 and 45.
For consolidation of both letter shape and sound use:
  – *Early Years Workbook 4*, pages 4-5.
  – *Letterland Phonics Online*.

Things to talk about

- **Up** Ask the children to think about the word up. We get up out of bed, go up the road/hill, climb up trees/stairs, look up, pick up, use up, fix up, hold up, step up, turn up, build up, keep up, mix up, sew up, grow up, wind up, etc. Help everyone to notice how often the word up comes up in the course of the week.

- **Under** Think about the word under with the children. Ask what we can go under, such as blankets, tables, bridges, trees, the sun, moon, stars, etc.

Explaining the capital U shape

Like everyone else in Letterland, Uppy Umbrella loves starting important words. Like them, all she has to do to get bigger is to take a deep breath. Talk about what it would be like if we could do this too.

Introducing Mr U, the Uniform Man

Show the children the picture of Mr U, the Uniform Man, on either the *Alphabet Frieze* or on the *Big Picture Code Cards*. Explain that Mr U has the important job of looking after all the umbrellas in Letterland. He must be important, as he always wears a uniform.

Mr U's words

unicorn
uniform
united
use
useful

---

dry so that the rain falls on the **u**mbrella, and not me! The Letterland queen uses her **u**mbrella as a sunshade as well.

Look at our bright Letterland **u**mbrella. Can you see her colours? Let's point to the colours. There's red, blue, yellow, green, red. What a cheerful **u**mbrella. We call her **U**ppy **U**mbrella because we put her **u**p when it rains. Can you say her name with me? **U**ppy **U**mbrella!

Session 2: Uppy Umbrella's shape and sound

Shall we hold out our hands again and pretend that it's raining? What do we need for the rain? Yes, an **u**mbrella. Let's find our special Letterland **u**mbrella. Can you remember her name? Yes, her name is **U**ppy **U**mbrella.

Uppy **U**mbrella says 'ŭ..., ŭ..., ŭ...' for **u**mbrella, and 'ŭ...' for **u**p. Let's pretend to put her **u**p while we say her 'ŭ...' sound. Have your hand ready holding the **u**mbrella. Press the button, push it **u**p and we say 'ŭ...' for **U**ppy **U**mbrella.

Let's do it again. Hold the **u**mbrella, press the button and push it **u**p while we make her 'ŭ...' sound.

Her letter shape is her handle. Can you see? Are you ready to make her letter shape? We're going to start at the top by her **u**mbrella. We're going to go *down* **u**nder, go *up* to the top and *down* again to stop it tipping over. Let's do it again while we say **U**ppy **U**mbrella's 'ŭ...' sound. Start at the top by her **u**mbrella. Go *down* under, and *up* to the top and *down* again, and we say 'ŭ...' for **U**ppy **U**mbrella.

Vicky Violet

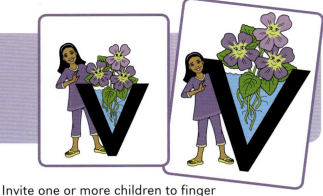

Objective

To teach the letter shapes and sound for **v** and **V**.

What you need

Letterland materials

- *Big Picture Code Cards*: VickyViolet
- *A-Z Copymasters*: **v** and **Vv**
- *Early Years Handwriting Copymasters*: 22 and 46
- *Early Years Workbook 4*: pages 6-7
- *Letterland Phonics Online*: **Vv**

Other materials

- Violet and green tissue paper
- Pipe cleaners
- Vase
- Vegetables
- Vanilla pod
- Vanilla ice cream
- African violet or real violets
- Velvet and other contrasting fabrics
- Toy vans

Teaching suggestions

Introducing Vicky Violet

Show the children the picture of Vicky Violet and her Vase of Violets on page 49 of the *ABC Book* and introduce her using the sample script for **Session 1** (shown right) as a guide for what to say. Invite one or more children to find and touch Vicky Violet and her vase on the *Alphabet Frieze*.

Vicky Violet's letter shape

Introduce **Session 2**. Then sing or chant the handwriting verse shown below (as on the *Handwriting Songs CD* or *Letterland Living ABC*) to help teach Vicky Violet's letter shape:

Very neatly, start at the top.
Draw down your vase, then up and stop.

Invite one or more children to finger trace Vicky Violet's letter shape on the *ABC Book* or on both sides of the *Big Picture Code Card*.

Vicky Violet's sound

The trick here again is to avoid an 'uh' sound, in this case by keeping teeth on lips while prolonging the '**vvv**...' sound. Look out for children who substitute '**fff**...' for '**vvv**...'. Vicky Violet's song on the *Alphabet Songs CD* or *Phonics Online* software will help children to achieve the correct sound.

Vicky Violet's words

valley	vet
van	village
vanilla	violets
vanish	violin
vase	visit
vegetables	visitor
velvet	voice
very	volcano
vest	vole

Vicky Violet's sample script

Session 1: Introducing Vicky Violet

What a lovely **V**ase of **V**iolets! We even call that colour **v**iolet. So the colour is **v**iolet and those flowers are called **v**iolets as well. The girl standing next to this lovely **V**ase of **V**iolets is called **V**icky **V**iolet. It is **V**icky's **V**ase of **V**iolets.

When you say the '**vvv**...' sound, it makes your lips tremble. We call it **v**ibrating. You say it with me. Ready? '**Vvv**..., **vvv**..., **V**icky's **V**ase of **V**iolets.' Did you feel your lip **v**ibrating, making that trembly feeling?

These **v**iolets are **v**ery special. They have five

Things to do

- **Making violets** Help to make violets by wrapping violet tissue paper around pipe cleaners for petals. For each violet, tie on five tissue paper leaves (good counting practice). Add the children's names to them. Make a display, perhaps in one or more vases. At the end of the week, everyone can take their violets home with them.
  [PSRN: Count reliably up to 10 everyday objects...]

- **Vegetable soup** Ask each child to bring in some vegetables on the day that you do **Session 2**. Let the children watch while you chop up vegetables to make vegetable soup. Encourage them to taste various raw vegetables before they are cooked. Serve the same day, or if need be, cook later and serve the next day. See the *Letterland Cookbook* for a great vegetable soup recipe!
  [KU: Find out about, and identify some features of, living things, objects...]

- **Vanilla** If possible, show the children a vanilla pod, and let them eat some vanilla ice cream.
  [CD: Respond in a variety of ways...]

- **Vanished!** Before the children arrive, remove one item or piece of furniture that is always in the room. See who can work out what has vanished.
  [KU: Observe, find out about, and identify features in the place they live...]

- **Further practice** Options for letter shapes:
  – *A-Z Copymasters:* **v** and **Vv**
  – *Early Years Handwriting Copymasters:* 22 and 46.
  For consolidation of both letter shape and sound use:
  – *Early Years Workbook 4*, pages 6-7.
  – *Letterland Phonics Online*.

Things to talk about

- **Violets** Bring in a pot of African violets, or real violets if possible. Talk about how different flowers grow in only certain colours, for example, buttercups and dandelions are always yellow. Violets can be bluish or white, but most violets are a shade of purple which we call '**violet**' after the flowers themselves.

- **Velvet** Talk about different kinds of cloth. Bring in a piece of velvet for the children to feel and compare with other materials.

- **Voices** Talk about our voices and explore the range of sounds the children can make. Practise both the vowel sounds ('**a**...', '**e**...', '**i**...', '**o**...' and '**u**...') and the vowel names ('**a**...', '**e**...', '**i**...', '**o**...' and '**u**...').

- **Vets** Talk about a vet's job (as an 'animal doctor') and ask if anyone has been to a vet with their own pet.

- **Vans** Talk about the various things that might be carried in a van or who might use one. If available, show the children some toy vans, e.g. a breakdown van, delivery van, etc.

- **Very good** Use very good as your main words of praise during your Vicky Violet week.

Explaining the capital V shape

Ask the children why some vases look bigger than others. Explain to them that in Letterland, children bring them nearer to us to show that the word starting with the big vase is an important word.

---

petals. One, two, at the top. Three, four and five, at the bottom.

I can see a little **v**ole nibbling some things in the corner of this picture. What is he nibbling? **V**egetables. Listen. **V**egetables. Did you hear the '**vvv**...' sound that **V**ase of **V**iolets makes at the beginning of that word? **V**egetables, **v**iolets in a **v**ase and a little **v**ole. All these words begin with **V**icky **V**iolet's letter.

Session 2: Vicky Violet's shape and sound

What a beautiful **v**ase for **V**icky's **v**iolets to sit in. Let's say her name together. **V**icky **V**iolet.

Did you feel your lips **v**ibrating when you made the '**vvv**...' sound for **V**icky **V**iolet? Let's say it again: **V**icky **V**iolet.

We can draw **V**icky **V**iolet's **v**ase. We start at the side, go *down* to the bottom of the **v**ase and back up the other side. Are you ready? Start at the side, go *down* to the bottom, and back up again. And we'll say '**vvv**..., **vvv**..., **vvv**...' while we do it.

Can you remember how many petals the **v**iolet has? Yes, it has five petals. One, two at the top, and three, four, fi**v**e at the bottom. We can feel the '**vvv**...' sound **v**ibrating at the end of the word fi**v**e. I'll close our book carefully. I must not knock over **V**icky's **V**ase of **V**iolets.

Walter Walrus

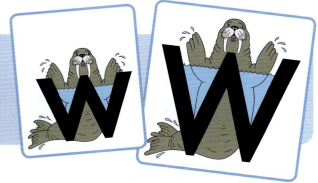

Objective

To teach the letter shapes and sound for **w** and **W**.

What you need

Letterland materials

- *Big Picture Code Cards*: Walter Walrus and any short vowel card except **u**
- *A-Z Copymasters*: **w** and **Ww**
- *Early Years Handwriting Copymasters*: 23 and 47
- *Early Years Workbook 4*: pages 8-9
- *Letterland Phonics Online*: **Ww**

Other materials

- Cardboard
- Cotton wool
- Black sticky tape
- One or more candles
- Corks
- Jar with a lid

Teaching suggestions

Introducing Walter Walrus

Show the children Walter Walrus on page 51 of the *Letterland ABC Book* and introduce him using the sample script for **Session 1** (shown right) as a guide for what to say. Invite one or more children to find and touch Walter Walrus on the *Letterland Alphabet Frieze*. Ask the children to point to the pools of water in his two wells.

Walter Walrus's letter shapes

Introduce **Session 2**. Then sing or chant the handwriting verse shown below (as on the *Handwriting Songs CD* or *Letterland Living ABC*) to help teach Walter Walrus's letter shape:

**When you draw the Walrus wells,
with wild and wavy water,
whizz down and up and then...,
whizz down and up again.**

Invite one or more children to finger trace Walter Walrus's letter shape on the *Letterland ABC Book* or on both sides of the *Big Picture Code Card*.

Walter Walrus's sound

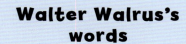

The children will need to avoid adding an 'uh' sound by keeping their lips pursed until after finishing the sound. Try practising the sound together with a vowel by holding *Big Picture Code Cards* of **w** and a short vowel side by side. Walter Walrus's song on the *Alphabet Songs CD* or *Letterland Phonics Online* will also help in achieving the correct sound.

Walter Walrus's words

walk	wax	win
want	we	wind
warm	week	window
wash	well	winter
water	wet	wish
wave	whale	with
way	what	word

Walter Walrus sample script

Session 1: Introducing Walter Walrus

Well, look who is **w**allowing near the Letterland **w**aterfall. It's **W**alter **W**alrus! **W**alter **W**alrus is resting with his **w**ebbed flippers **w**edged into his two **w**ater **w**ells while he sunbathes.

Walter **W**alrus is having a **w**onderful time **w**atching the **w**hales and all the other animals who have come to see the **w**aterfall. There's a **w**olf, two **w**easels, a **w**ombat, a **w**oodpecker and another **w**alrus. **W**alter **W**alrus will make them all **w**et with **w**ater from his two **w**ater **w**ells before long! And all the animals will hear him making his low '**www**...' sound.

Things to do

- **Wave patterns** Cut out a cardboard 'comb' for the children to make wavy patterns with, using a plateful of finger paints.
  [CLL: Attempt writing for various purposes...]

- **Winter pictures** The children can stick white paper hills and cotton wool snowmen on to coloured paper to make winter scenes. Add a window frame to the pictures using black tape.
  [KU: Look closely at similarities, differences...]

- **Wax beetles** Beforehand, drip drops of candle wax on to paper to make raised blobs. The children can then add six legs and eyes with paint or crayons to make wax beetles.
  [PSRN: Count reliably up to 10 everyday objects.]

- **Sinking or floating?** Put a closed empty jar into a bowl of water to see if it floats. First ask the children if it will sink. Add some water and ask if it will still float. Find out together how much water will make it sink. Let them experiment to see what else will sink or float.
  [KU: Investigate objects and materials by using...]

- **Further practice** Options for letter shapes:
  – *A-Z Copymasters*: **w** and **Ww**
  – *Early Years Handwriting Copymasters*: 23 and 47.
  For consolidation of both letter shape and sound use:
  – *Early Years Workbook 4*, pages 8-9.
  – *Letterland Phonics Online*. Make use of your whiteboard to introduce Walter Walrus to the class.

Things to talk about

- **Winners and losers** Talk about being good winners and good losers, and how to do it.

- **Days of the week** Find out if everyone knows the names of all seven days of the week. Learn them off by heart together. Ask which day of the week will be Walter Walrus's favourite (**Wednesday**).

- **Wishing** Tell the children that Walter Walrus wishes that his water wells were a bit warmer. Ask what they would like if they could make a wish.

- **Road signs** Suggest that the children look out for 'water wells' on road signs. Describe the GIVE WAY sign and explain where to find such signs.

- **Favourite foods** Help the children to think of Walter Walrus's favourite foods. He is a Letterland walrus so he likes things that begin with his sound, such as **waffles** and **wine gums**.

- **Knowing why** See page 19.

Explaining the capital W shape

Explain that when Walter Walrus takes a deep breath, his letter gets bigger. It even holds more water! He always makes his letter bigger when he has a chance to start an important word, like somebody's name.

Can you see a pink **w**indmill in the picture? What makes the sails go round on a **w**indmill? Yes, the **w**ind does. And when there's no **w**ind at all, the sails will be still, won't they?

What would happen to the **w**ater on a very **w**indy day? There would be lots of **w**aves, and all the Letterlanders would want to **w**indsurf on the **w**ater! I **w**onder whether we'd still hear Walter **W**alrus's low '**www**...' sound in the **www**ind and the **www**aves?

Session 2: Walter Walrus's shape and sound

Can you remember this **w**alrus's name? Yes, we call him **W**alter **W**alrus, don't we? Can you hear his '**www**...' sound when I say his name? **Www**alter **Www**alrus. Look, his letter holds the **w**ater in his two **w**ater **w**ells, with one **w**ell on each side.

Walter **W**alrus makes a sound in **w**ords which is like **w**ind blowing. '**Www**...', he says, '**Www**..., **www**..., **www**...'. Can you make **W**alter **W**alrus's **w**indy sound?

Let's see if we can draw the side of his **w**ells. Are you ready? We start at this side above his first **w**ell. We go *down*, up and *down*, up again. Let's try once more and we'll say his sound while we do it. Start by his first **w**ell, go *down*, up and *down*, up while we make **W**alter **W**alrus's '**www**...' sound.

Fix-it Max

Objective

To teach the letter shapes and sound for **x** and **X**.

What you need

Letterland materials

- *Big Picture Code Cards*: Fix-it Max
- *A-Z Copymasters*: **x** and **Xx**
- *Early Years Handwriting Copymasters*: 24 and 47
- *Early Years Workbook 4*: pages 10-11
- *Letterland Phonics Online*: **Xx**

Other materials

- Sandpaper
- White or yellow wax crayons or candles
- Paper, card and glue
- Icing sugar
- Cake ingredients

Teaching suggestions

Introducing Fix-it Max

Show the children the picture of Fix-it Max on page 53 of the *Letterland ABC Book* and introduce him using the sample script for **Session 1** (shown right) as a guide for what to say. Invite one or more children to find and touch Fix-it Max on the *Letterland Alphabet Frieze* and to find and touch his capital letter shape, as well.

Fix-it Max's letter shape

Introduce **Session 2**. Then sing or chant the handwriting verse shown below (as on the *Handwriting Songs CD* or *Letterland Living ABC*) to help teach Fix-it Max's letter shape:

Fix two sticks, to look like this.
That's how to draw a little kiss.

Invite one or more children to finger trace Max's letter shape on the *Letterland ABC Book* or on both sides of the *Big Picture Code Card*.

Fix-it Max's sound

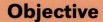

This sound is tricky because it is really two sounds: '**k**' + '**s**'. That is why it helps to whisper the word '**k...ss**'. Try whispering all the words in **Fix-it Max's words** (see below) with the children. Fix-it Max's song on the *Alphabet Songs* or *Phonics Online* will also help in achieving the correct sound.

Fix-it Max's words

box	next
exit	six
fix	sixteen
fox	sixty
mix	taxi
mixture	wax

Fix-it Max sample script

Session 1: Introducing Fix-it Max

This si**x**-year-old boy likes to fi**x** things. That's why everyone in Letterland calls him Fi**x**-it Ma**x**. Can you say 'Ma**x**' for me? He is in his workshop with all his tools. He loves spending time in his workshop. The Letterlanders are always bringing Ma**x** their broken things for him to fi**x**. This is his cousin Ma**x**ine. Ma**x**ine is stroking a lovely brown fo**x**. Most fo**x**es live in the wild, but this fo**x** has become a pet. Ma**x** is going to fi**x** him up with a nice new kennel to sleep in.

Right now Fix-it Max is just about to fi**x** this broken E**X**IT sign. Then he wants to fi**x** Eddy

Things to do

- **X pictures** Help the children to cut strips of sandpaper and glue them in six **x**-shapes on to a piece of card or stiff paper. The children then shut their eyes and finger trace the **x**'s while counting to six. When they open their eyes they can point as they say 'kss' six times.
  [CD: Respond in a variety of ways...]

- **Wax resist** Help the children to draw **x**-shapes on pieces of paper with a white or yellow wax crayon (or a candle). Then let them paint the paper completely with watery black or blue paint. Watch together as the **x**'s disappear under the paint and then appear again.
  [KU: Ask questions about why things happen...]

- **Crossroads** Using a road mat, plus some toy cars and toy people, show the children how to be careful at crossroads. Ask them to see how many crossroads they can count on the mat.
  [KU: Find out about, and identify some features...]

- **Kisses** Help children to make a card to parents or carers, and then to 'write' in it with love and kisses (**XXX**).
  [CLL: Attempt writing for various purposes...]

- **Cookery** Show the children how to ice **x**'s on to biscuits as kisses. They could also help to mix a cake.
  [KU: Look closely at similarities, diffferences...]

- **Further practice** Options for letter shapes:
  – *A-Z Copymasters:* **x** and **Xx**
  – *Early Years Handwriting Copymasters:* 24 and 47.
  For consolidation of both letter shape and sound use:
  – *Early Years Workbook 4,* pages 10-11.
  – *Letterland Phonics Online ABC.*

Things to talk about

- **EXIT signs** Make an EXIT sign to put over the door which the children use to leave the building. Talk about other places where they might look out for this sign, such as in shops, cinemas, etc. Get them to listen to Max's sound just after Eddy Elephant's sound in this word. Explain that Max's letter does not appear in many words. The children will have to look out for it inside words and at the end of words, because very few start with it. Find some words together, such as **fox**, **wax**, **fix** or even **chicken pox**!

- **Taxis** Talk about taxis and how or where you might find one. Explain that people might use a taxi if they do not have a car, or do not live near public transport. Ask if anyone has ridden in a taxi. Then try making up a story about Max and his best friend Maxine taking a taxi. They could see some **x**-words on their taxi ride, such as a **fox** crossing the road, some-body carrying **six** or **sixteen** boxes, a person **fixing** a car, etc.

- **Foxes** Max and Maxine have a pet fox. Talk about foxes, e.g. where they live, what they eat, etc. Explain that a female fox is called a **vixen**.

Explaining the capital X shape

Ask the children if they can guess how Fix-it Max makes his letter look bigger, like many of his friends in Letterland. (He just takes a deep breath.)

Elephant's e**x**ercise machine. Oh look! I can see Lucy Lamp Light through the window. She is carrying a broken lamp for Ma**x** to fi**x**.

When Ma**x** gives back things he has fi**x**ed he always adds a note saying, 'All fi**x**ed. Love and kisses.' For the kisses he just writes his letter. Did you know that's how you can send kisses on notes and birthday cards?

Session 2: Fix-it Max's shape and sound

Can you remember the name of these cousins? Yes, they are Fi**x**-it Ma**x** and his cousin Ma**x**ine.

Do you know what it means when people write Ma**x**'s letter at the end of a birthday card? It is a special way of sending kisses! Maybe that's why

the special sound that Ma**x** makes in words is just like the word 'kiss' said in a whisper. Let's all whisper it, '**k-ss**..., **k-ss**..., **k-ss**...'.

When we write Ma**x**'s letter, we start at his arm and go across his body and *down* to his foot – in the Reading Direction! Then we start at the top on his other side and go across his body to the other foot. His letter is just like two crossed sticks.

Let's say Ma**x**'s sound while we make his letter shape. Start here at the top, '**k-ss**..., **k-ss**...'. Good! Can you hear Ma**x**'s '**k-ss**...' sound at the end of his name? You can hear it at the end of the word fo**x**, too. And bo**x**. Let's all whisper Ma**x**'s sound again while we draw his letter in the air, '**k-ss**..., **k-ss**...'.

Yellow Yo-yo Man

Objective

To teach the letter shapes and sound for **y** and **Y**.

What you need

Letterland materials

- *Big Picture Code Cards*: Yellow Yo-yo Man, Eddy Elephant and Sammy Snake
- *A-Z Copymasters*: **y** and **Yy**
- *Early Years Handwriting Copymasters*: 25 and 48
- *Early Years Workbook 4*: pages 12-13
- *Letterland Phonics Online*: **Yy**

Other materials

- Yellow tissue paper
- Cardboard circles
- Polystyrene trays or corks
- Straws or cocktails sticks
- Yellow sack or bag and string
- Different flavoured yogurts
- Raw and cooked eggs

Teaching suggestions

Introducing Yellow Yo-yo Man

Show the children the picture of Yellow Yo-yo Man on page 55 of the *Letterland ABC Book* and introduce him using the sample script for **Session 1** (shown right) as a guide for what to say. Invite one or more children to find and touch Yo-yo Man on the *Letterland Alphabet Frieze*. Ask a child to find and touch the yellow yo-yos in his sack.

Yellow Yo-yo Man's letter shape

Introduce **Session 2**. Then sing or chant the handwriting verse shown below (as on *Handwriting Songs CD* or *Letterland Living ABC*) to help teach Yellow Yo-yo Man's letter shape:

**You first make the yo-yo sack
on the Yo-yo Man's back,
and then go down to his toes
so he can sell his yo-yos.**

Invite one or more children to finger trace Yo-yo Man's letter shape on the *ABC Book* or on both sides of the *Big Picture Code Card*.

Yellow Yo-yo Man's sound

The Yellow Yo-yo Man only makes his '**yyy**...' sound at the *start* of words. If asked, explain that at the *end* of words like **my**, he says, '**ī**...' for Mr I, and for words like **Daddy**, he says '**ē**...' for Mr E. The Yo-yo Man's song on the *Alphabet Songs CD* or *Phonics Online* will help in achieving the correct initial sound. Set out the *Big Picture Code Cards* to spell the word **yes** and teach this word to the children by showing how their sounds blend together: '**yyye**...**sss**'.

Yellow Yo-yo Man's words

yacht	yesterday
yawn	yo-yo
year	yogurt
yell	yolk
yellow	you
yes	your

Yellow Yo-yo Man sample script

Session 1: Introducing Yellow Yo-yo Man

Take a look at this man, all dressed in **y**ellow. What has he got on his back? Is it a sack? I wonder what is inside that sack? It's not a ball. It's not even a ball on a string. It looks like a ball on a string, doesn't it? It has a very special name. It's called a **y**o-**y**o.

If **y**ou are very clever, **y**ou can make a **y**o-**y**o go up and down the string, up and down. That's a **y**o-**y**o. I'm not very good at making the **y**o-**y**o go up and down the string. But this man is.

We call this man the **Y**ellow **Y**o-**y**o Man. He

Things to do

- **Yellow collection**
Ask everyone to bring in as many objects as possible that are yellow. Display them under a big painting of the Yo-yo Man or a collage made by crumpling and sticking on yellow tissue paper. Ask the children to try to wear or bring in something yellow during the week.
[CD: Explore colour, texture, shape...]

- **Yachts** Help the children to make yachts from junk, such as polystyrene trays, with masts from drinking straws and paper sails, or cocktail sticks with a small paper sail stuck into corks. Then they can race the yachts across a water tray, blowing hard.
[KU: Build and construct with a wide range...]

- **Yo-yo Man mime** The children can take turns in miming the Yo-yo Man getting up, yawning, getting dressed, filling his sack with yo-yos, setting off yelling 'Yyyo-yos for sale', and selling some to everyone.
[CD: Use their imagination in art and design...]

- **Food** Suggest the children try some different yoghurt flavours.
[CD: Respond in a variety of ways...]

- **Further practice** Options for letter shapes:
  – *A-Z Copymasters:* y and **Yy**
  – *Early Years Handwriting Copymasters:* 25 and 48.
For consolidation of both letter shape and sound use:
  – *Early Years Workbook 4*, pages 12-13.
  – *Letterland Phonics Online.*

Things to talk about

- **Yesterday** Make a list of things that you have done today. Go over them the next day stressing how they all happened yesterday. Repeat on several days.

- **Year** Tell the children that there are 365 days in the year. Ask them individually how many years old they are and how old their brother, sister, dog, etc. is. Talk about the seasons that make up the year.

- **Egg yolks** Look at egg yolks together and compare a cooked yolk with an uncooked yolk.

- **Young** Talk about young and old. Ask the children if they know someone very young or if there is someone younger than them in the family. Find out the names of young animals together, e.g. puppy, kitten, calf, lamb, etc.

- **Yaks** Many alphabets use a picture of a yak to represent the initial sound of **y**. Link the yak to the Yo-yo Man by explaining that he enjoys visiting the yaks at the Letterland zoo. The zoo keeper lets him feed the yaks there with special yellow yak food.

- **Yawning** Ask the children what we usually do every evening that the Yo-yo Man does as well. Explain that yawning can be catching. Get everyone to pretend to yawn and then see if they find themselves yawning again for real.

Explaining the capital Y shape

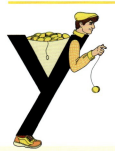

Tell the children that when the Yo-yo Man has a chance to be in an important word, he quickly empties out some of his yo-yos (which are heavy) so that he can step lightly up on to the line to show how important that word is.

has loads of **y**o-**y**os in his sack and he's dressed in **y**ellow. Let's look out for the **Y**ellow **Y**o-**y**o Man's letter in words.

Goodbye for now, **Y**ellow **Y**o-**y**o Man. We'll see **y**ou again soon. Goodbye, **Y**ellow **Y**o-**y**o Man.

Session 2: Yellow Yo-yo Man's shape and sound

Do **y**ou remember the name of this **y**ellow thing on a string? **Y**es, it's a **y**o-**y**o. Our friend here is called the **Y**ellow **Y**o-**y**o Man. Look at his long **y**ellow letter. Shall we make his letter?

Start at the outside of his sack, go *right* down it, up to his neck and *down* his long **y**ellow legs, bending his legs back up to his shoes. Ready? Let's

do it again and make his sound while we do it. It's a very quiet sound, '**yyy**..., **yyy**...' for **Y**o-**y**o Man.

Start at the outside of his sack, go *right* down, *up* to his neck and *down* his long **y**ellow legs, bending his legs back up to his shoes. Now let's all say '**yyy**..., **yyy**...' for **Y**o-**y**o Man. '**Yyy**...' for **y**ellow and '**yyy**...' for **y**o-**y**o.

Oh, there's a special boat on the sea by the **Y**o-**y**o Man. We can't call it a boat, because it has to start with **Y**o-**y**o Man's sound. Does anybody know what that special sort of boat is called? That's right. It's a **y**acht. A **y**acht always has big sails like that to catch the wind. **Y**acht starts with **Y**ellow **Y**o-**y**o Man's '**yyy**...' sound.

Zig Zag Zebra

Objective

To teach the letter shapes and sound for **z** and **Z**.

What you need

Letterland materials

- *Big Picture Code Cards*: Zig Zag Zebra
- *A-Z Copymasters*: **z** and **Zz**
- *Early Years Handwriting Copymasters*: 26 and 48
- *Early Years Workbook 4*: pages 14-15
- *Letterland Phonics Online*: **Zz**

Other materials

- Black and white paper
- Small toy animals
- Pictures of rare zoo animals
- Toy model zoo (if available)
- Zips
- Toy or model rocket
- Orange or lemon
- Peeler or zester
- Ingredients for cakes or biscuits

Teaching suggestions

Introducing Zig Zag Zebra

Show the children the picture of Zig Zag Zebra on page 57 of the *Letterland ABC Book* and introduce her using the sample script for **Session 1** (shown right) as a guide for what to say. Invite one or more children to find and touch Zig Zag Zebra on the *Letterland Alphabet Frieze*. Ask them how she looks when she starts important words.

Zig Zag Zebra's letter shape

Introduce **Session 2**. Sing or chant the handwriting verse shown below (*Handwriting Songs CD or software*) to help teach Zig Zag Zebra's letter shape:

Zip along Zig Zag's nose.
Stroke her neck...,
stroke her back... Zzzoom!
Away she goes.

Invite one or more children to finger trace Zig Zag Zebra's letter shape on the *Letterland ABC Book* or on both sides of the *Big Picture Code Cards*.

Zig Zag Zebra's sound

This is an easy sound to learn and is fun to practise. The children may like to make four fingers gallop while they all say '**zzz**...' together. Further practice can also be found by listening to Zig Zag Zebra's song on the *Alphabet Songs CD* or the *Letterland Phonics Online*.

> ### Zig Zag Zebra's words
>
> crazy
> dizzy
> fizzy
> lazy
> puzzle
> zebra
> zebra crossing
> zero
> zip
> zoo
> zoom

Zig Zag Zebra sample script

Session 1: Introducing Zig Zag Zebra

Who have I got here? A **z**ebra. This is **Z**ig **Z**ag **Z**ebra. Look at her **z**ig **z**ag body and her **z**ig **z**ag stripes.

    Zig **Z**ag **Z**ebra doesn't live in a park. Where do you think she lives? Yes, that's right. She lives in the Letterland **z**oo.

    Zig **Z**ag **Z**ebra likes to **z**oom around the **z**oo as fast as she can go. How many other animals in the **z**oo do you think can run as fast as **Z**ig **Z**ag **Z**ebra? **Z**ero! That means none, not even one!

Things to do

- **Zebra crossing** Make a zebra crossing by taping strips of black and white paper together, or by pouring water on to paving stones to make a striped effect. Then use it to practise care in crossing the road. Stress that even with a zebra crossing, children should never cross the road alone and never run into the road.
  [KU: Observe, find out about, and identify features...]

- **Zoo animals** Ask the children to bring in small toy animals and include pictures of rare zoo animals, if possible. Sort them into zoo animals, farm animals and perhaps also indoor and outdoor pets. If a toy model zoo is available, use it for play activities, or use model farm fences to create enclosures.
  [KU: Find out about, and identify some features...]

- **Zoo play** Mark out and label different areas for zoo animals. Appoint one or several children as 'zoo keepers'. Let the other children choose which animals to be. The 'zoo keepers' can mime feeding the animals, including Zig Zag Zebra.
  [CD: Use their imagination in art, design...]

- **Being zebras** Help the children to make black and white ears from card or stiff paper and attach them to card headbands. They can also make and wear black and white tails. The 'zebras' can gallop about outside, practising '**zzz**...' sounds.
  [CD: Use their imagination in art, design...]

- **Further practice** Options for letter shapes:
  – *A-Z Copymasters:* **z** and **Zz**
  – *Early Years Handwriting Copymasters:* 26 and 48.
  For consolidation of both letter shape and sound use:
  – *Early Years Workbook 4*, pages 14-15.
  – *Letterland Phonics Online*.

Things to talk about

- **Zebras** Talk about their stripes, where they live, and the kinds of animals that live with them: antelopes, gazelles, wildebeests, lions, leopards, etc.

- **Zips** Talk about how zips work and practise using them on clothes or other items. Point out how the word **zip** and other words, such as **zoom**, **sizzle** and **fizzy** are closely related to the sounds they make. Explain that Zig Zag Zebra loves being in words that come from special sounds!

- **Zero** Talk about the word **zero** and its meaning. Do a countdown together, ten to zero and blast off, if possible with a toy or model rocket.

- **Zest** Scrape lemon or orange peel while explaining that it is also called the **zest**. Use it later in a biscuit dough or cake mixture for baking and eating.

Explaining the capital Z shape

Explain that when Zig Zag Zebra has a chance to start an important word, she takes a deep breath and gets bigger. We don't see her looking big (or small) very often in words, however, because she is very shy.

Zig Zag Zebra runs so fast, she makes all the other animals feel di**zz**y. When she is not **z**ooming around, Zig Zag Zebra sometimes closes her eyes and has a snoo**z**e under the trees.

What other animals can you see in the **z**oo?

Session 2: Zig Zag Zebra's shape and sound

I know you'll remember our **z**ebra's name. Her black and white stripes and her special shape will remind you. Yes, it's **Z**ig **Z**ag **Z**ebra.

Just look how her letter **z**ig **z**ags when we draw it. I'm going to start by her nose and I'm going to **z**ig **z**ag from her head *right* down to her tail.

Let's do it again. Ready? Start by her nose and **z**ig **z**ag down to her tail.

Do you like doing up **z**ips? I do, and I like to say '**zzz**ip!' as I **zzz**ip it up. I like saying **zzz**ig **zzz**ag, too. Do you?

Now let's just *start* to say **Z**ig **Z**ag **Z**ebra's name. That's how we can remember the little '**zzz**...' sound she makes in words. **Z**ig **Z**ag **Z**ebra says '**zzz**...'.

The Alphabet Songs

Available on the *Alphabet Songs CD* or *Letterland Phonics Online*.

Familiar nursery tunes are a popular and effective vehicle for Letterland verses which practise each letter's sound. Before singing a particular song, a leader, who could be the teacher or a child, can hold up the appropriate *Big Picture Code Card*, plain side first, then the pictogram side, and then announce the character's name. Where a letter has a voiceless sound, i.e. in the case of **c**, **f**, **h**, **k**, **p**, **q**, **s**, **t** and **x**, make sure the children sing it in a whisper.

Annie Apple

(To the tune of London Bridge is falling down)
Annie Apple, she says 'ă...',
she says 'ă...', she says 'ă...'.
Annie Apple, she says 'ă...'.
She belongs to Mr A.

Bouncy Ben

(To the tune of Polly put the kettle on)
Bouncy Ben says '**b**...' in words.
Bouncy Ben says '**b**...' in words.
Bouncy Ben says '**b**...' in words,
before he bounces home.

Clever Cat

(To the tune of Merrily we roll along)
Clever Cat says '**c**...' in words,
'**c**...' in words, '**c**...' in words.
Clever Cat says '**c**...' in words,
and cuddles close to me.

She also makes another sound,
another sound, another sound.
She also makes another sound.
Just you wait and see.

Dippy Duck

(To the tune of Hey, diddle diddle)
Dippy Duck, Dippy Duck,
We never hear her quack.
She says '**d**... **d**...' instead.
The little duck dips and dives about,
as the water drips over her head.

Eddy Elephant

(To the tune of Oh the grand old
Duke of York)
Here comes Eddy El-e-phant
to talk to you and me.
He just says 'ĕ...', he just says 'ĕ...'.
He belongs to Mr E.

Firefighter Fred

(To the tune of Here we go round the
mulberry bush)
Firefighter Fred goes '**fff**..., **fff**..., **fff**...',
Firefighter Fred, Firefighter Fred.
Firefighter Fred goes '**fff**..., **fff**..., **fff**...',
fighting fires with foam.

Golden Girl

(To the tune of Merrily we roll along)
Golden Girl says '**g**...' in words,
'**g**...' in words, '**g**...' in words.
Golden Girl says '**g**...' in words,
giggling merrily.

Her girlfriend makes another sound,
another sound, another sound.
Her girlfriend makes another sound.
Just you wait and see.

Harry Hat Man

(To the tune of The wheels on the bus)
Harry Hat Man whispers '**hhh**...',
whispers '**hhh**...', whispers '**hhh**...'.

Harry Hat Man whispers '**hhh**...'.
He never talks out loud.

Impy Ink

(To the tune of London Bridge is falling down)
Impy Ink says '**ĭ**...' in words,
'**ĭ**...' in words, '**ĭ**...' in words.
Impy Ink says '**ĭ**...' in words.
He belongs to Mr I.

Jumping Jim

(To the tune of Old MacDonald had a farm)
Jumping Jim says '**j**...' in words,
as he jumps along.
Jumping Jim says '**j**...' in words,
as he jumps along.
With a '**j**..., **j**...' here, and a '**j**..., **j**...' there;
here a '**j**...', there a '**j**...',
everywhere a '**j**..., **j**...'.
Jumping Jim says '**j**...' in words,
as he jumps along.

Kicking King

(To the tune of Merrily we roll along)
Kicking King says '**k**...' in words,
'**k**...' in words, '**k**...' in words.
Kicking King says '**k**...' in words,
as he kicks along.

Lucy Lamp Light

(To the tune of Twinkle, twinkle, little star)
Look, look, look, that lovely light.
It is Lucy's light so bright.
Listen, '**lll**...' is what she'll say,
'**Lll**...' for lamp, both night and day.
Look, look, look, that lovely light.
It is Lucy's light so bright.

Munching Mike

(To the tune of Humpty Dumpty)
'**Mmm**...', that monster Munching Mike.
My, he has an appetite.
'**Mmm**...', he hums contentedly,
munching mouthfuls merrily.

Noisy Nick

(To the tune of Here we go round the mulberry bush)
Noisy Nick says '**nnn**...' in words,
'**nnn**...' in words, '**nnn**...' in words.
Noisy Nick says '**nnn**...' in words.
You can hear it nnnow!

Oscar Orange

(To the tune of Polly put the kettle on)
Oscar Orange, he says '**ŏ**...'.
Oscar Orange, he says '**ŏ**...'.
Oscar Orange, he says '**ŏ**...'.
He belongs to Mr O.

Peter Puppy

(To the tune of The wheels on the bus)
Peter Puppy just says '**p**...',
just says '**p**...', just says '**p**...'.
Peter Puppy just says '**p**...',
his poor ears droop.

Quarrelsome Queen

(To the tune of Here we go round the mulberry bush)
Quarrelsome Queen says '**qu**...' in words,
'**qu**...' in words, '**qu**...' in words.
Quarrelsome Queen says '**qu**...' in words.
She must have her umbrella.

Red Robot

(To the tune of Three blind mice)
Red Ro-bot, Red Ro-bot.
See how he runs. See how he runs.
He rrreally makes a growling sound.
He's always heard, but he's never found.
Have you ever seen such a rascal around!
'**Rrr**..., **rrr**..., **rrr**...'.

Sammy Snake

(To the tune of Sing a song of sixpence)
Sammy Snake says '**sss**...' in words,
hissing all the time.
Sammy Snake says '**sss**...' in words,
hissing all the time.
Hissing with a '**sss**..., **sss**...',
hissing with a '**sss**...'
Sammy Snake says '**sss**...' in words,
he's hissing all the time.

Talking Tess

(To the tune of Old MacDonald had a farm)
Talking Tess says '**t**...' in words,
talking all the time.
Talking Tess says '**t**...' in words,
talking all the time.
With a '**t**..., **t**...' here and a '**t**..., **t**...' there;
here a '**t**...', there a '**t**...',
everywhere a '**t**..., **t**...'
Talking Tess says '**t**...' in words,
talking all the time.

Uppy Umbrella

(To the tune of Here we go round the mulberry bush)
Uppy Umbrella says '**ŭ**...' in words,
'**ŭ**...' in words, '**ŭ**...' in words.
Uppy Umbrella says '**ŭ**...' in words.
She belongs to Mr U.

Vicky Violet

(To the tune of Twinkle, twinkle, little star)
Vicky's Vase of Vi-o-lets.
Lovely Vase of Vi-o-lets.
The sound they make in words is '**vvv**...'.
The sound they make in words is '**vvv**...'.
Vicky's Vase of Vi-o-lets.
Lovely Vase of Vi-o-lets.

Walter Walrus

(To the tune of Polly put the kettle on)
'**Www**...' '**www**...', what's that we hear?
Is Walter Walrus near?

'**Www**...' '**www**...', yes, that's him!
You may get wet, I fear!

Fix-it Max

(To the tune of Old MacDonald had a farm)
Now let's whisper, whisper '**k-ss**',
whisper, whisper '**k-ss**'.
Now let's whisper, whisper '**k-ss**',
whisper, whisper '**k-ss**'.
With a '**k-ss**', '**k-ss**' here
and a '**k-ss**', '**k-ss**' there;
here a '**k-ss**', there a '**k-ss**',
everywhere a '**k-ss**', '**k-ss**'.
Now let's whisper, whisper '**k-ss**',
whisper, whisper '**k-ss**'.

Yellow Yo-yo Man

(To the tune of Baa, baa, black sheep)
Yo-yo Man says '**yyy**...' in words.
Yyyes sir, yes sir, '**yyy**...' in words.
Yellow yo-yos he will sell,
and work for other men as well.

Zig Zag Zebra

(To the tune of Humpty Dumpty)
Zig Zag Zebra is very shy,
saying '**zzz**...' while zzzipping by.
Zebras often seem to be shy,
but we'll never really know why.

Vowel Sounds Song

I am Annie Apple.
I am a talking apple.
I say '**ă**..., **ă**..., **ă**...',
I say '**ă**..., **ă**..., **ă**...'.

We are the vowel sounds.
There are lots of us around.
In fact, have you heard:
we're in almost every word.

I am Eddy Elephant.
I am a talking elephant.
I say '**ĕ**..., **ĕ**..., **ĕ**...',
I say '**ĕ**..., **ĕ**..., **ĕ**...'.

We are the vowel sounds.
There are lots of us around.
In fact, have you heard:
we're in almost every word.

I am Impy Ink.
I am a talking ink bottle.
I say 'ĭ..., ĭ..., ĭ...',
I say 'ĭ..., ĭ..., ĭ...'.

We are the vowel sounds.
There are lots of us around.
In fact, have you heard:
we're in almost every word.

I am Oscar Orange.
I am a talking orange.
I say 'ŏ..., ŏ..., ŏ...',
I say 'ŏ..., ŏ..., ŏ...'.

We are the vowel sounds.
There are lots of us around.
In fact, have you heard:
we're in almost every word.

I am Uppy Umbrella.
I am a talking umbrella.
I say 'ŭ..., ŭ..., ŭ...',
I say 'ŭ..., ŭ..., ŭ...'.

We are the vowel sounds.
There are lots of us around.
In fact, have you heard:
we're in almost every word.
Oh, all five of us are vowel sounds
and there's lots of us around.

Vowel Men Song

I am a Vowel Man.
My name is Mr A.
I wear an apron,
an apron everyday.
All five of us are Vowel Men,
and I am Mr A!
All five of us are Vowel Men,
and I am Mr A!
I am a Vowel Man.

My name is Mr E.
My magic tricks
are marvellous to see.
All five of us are Vowel Men,
and I am Mr E!
All five of us are Vowel Men,
and I am Mr E!

I am a Vowel Man,
My name is Mr I.
I sell ice cream
for you to come and buy.
All five of us are Vowel Men,
and I am Mr I!
All five of us are Vowel Men,
and I am Mr I!

I am a Vowel Man.
My name is Mr O.
I am an old man
but I'm still full of go.
All five of us are Vowel Men,
and I am Mr O!
All five of us are Vowel Men,
and I am Mr O!

I am a Vowel Man.
My name is Mr U.
I have a uniform,
a uniform that's blue.
All five of us are Vowel Men,
and I am Mr U!
All five of us are Vowel Men,
and I am Mr U!

We're glad to meet you.
We hope you understand:
you are all welcome
here in Letterland!
Oh, all of you are welcome
here in Letterland.

The Handwriting Songs

Available on the *Handwriting Songs CD* or the *Letterland Phonics Online*.

Words by Lyn Wendon and Vivien Stone

Annie Apple

At the leaf begin.
Go round the apple this way.
Then add a line down,
so Annie won't roll away.

Bouncy Ben

Brush down Ben's big, long ears.
Go up and round his head
so his face appears!

Clever Cat

Curve round Clever Cat's face to begin.
Then gently tickle her under her chin.

Dippy Duck

Draw Dippy Duck's back.
Go round her tum.
Go up to her head.
Then down you come!

Eddy Elephant

Ed has a headband.
Draw it and then
stroke round his head
and his trunk to the end.

Firefighter Fred

First draw Fred's helmet.
Then go down a way.
Give him some arms
and he'll put out the blaze.

Golden Girl

Go round Golden Girl's head.
Go down her golden hair.
Then curve to make her swing,
so she can sit there.

Harry Hat Man

Hurry from the Hat Man's head
down to his heel on the ground.
Go up and bend his knee over,
so he'll hop while he makes his sound.

Impy Ink

Inside the ink bottle draw a line.
Add an inky dot. That's fine!

Jumping Jim

Just draw down Jim, bending his knees.
Then add the one ball
which everyone sees.

Kicking King

Kicking King's body is a straight stick.
Add his arm, then his leg, so he can kick!

Lucy Lamp Light

Lucy looks like one long line.
Go straight from head to foot
and she's ready to shine!

Munching Mike

Make Munching Mike's back leg first,
then his second leg, and third,
so he can go munch-munching in a word.

Noisy Nick

'Now bang my nail,' Noisy Nick said.
'Go up and over around my head.'

Oscar Orange

On Oscar Orange start at the top.
Go all the way round him, and... then stop.

Peter Puppy

Pat Peter Puppy properly.
First stroke down his ear,
then up and round his face
so he won't shed a tear.

Quarrelsome Queen

Quickly go round the Queen's cross face.
Then comb her beautiful hair into place.

Red Robot

Run down Red Robot's body.
Go up to his arm and his hand.
Then watch out for this robot
roaming round Letterland.

Sammy Snake

Start at Sam's head
where he can see.
Stroke down to his tail, oh so care-ful-ly!

Talking Tess

Tall as a tower make Talking Tess stand.
Go from head to toe,
and then from hand to hand.
Uppy Umbrella
Under the umbrella
draw a shape like a cup.
Then draw a straight line
so it won't tip up.

Vicky Violet

Very neatly, start at the top.
Draw down your vase, then up and stop.

Walter Walrus

When you draw the Walrus wells,
with wild and wavy water,
whizz down and up and then...,
whizz down and up again.

Fix-it Max

Fix two sticks, to look like this.
That's how to draw a little kiss.

Yellow Yo-yo Man

You first make the yo-yo sack
on the Yo-yo Man's back,
and then go down to his toes
so he can sell his yo-yos.

Zig Zag Zebra

Zip along Zig Zag's nose.
Stroke her neck...,
stroke her back...
Zzzoom! Away she goes.

The Action Tricks

Objective

To develop visual, auditory, kinesthetic and tactile memory cues for letter sounds.

Teaching

Learning a sound together with an action activates mind and body simultaneously. Each action triggers an ideational link to the letter character or its shape.

Explain to the children that each Letterlander has given us an action to help us remember their letter sound. To begin with, encourage children to *make the sound each time they make the action*, so that the action and sound become firmly associated. Later on you could try just the actions in various activities. For example:

- A child makes an action and the rest of the class says the corresponding sound.
- Children play an Actions Game where they make each action in alphabetical order.
- Children spell a simple three-letter word using actions only. The others convert the actions into sounds to build the word.

The ACTION TRICKS
The actions are designed to be performed either sitting or standing. Where relevant, children should be facing in the Reading Direction. A full colour poster of the actions is available from **www.letterland.com**.

a Bite an imaginary apple.	**b** Shoot arms up for ears and wiggle them.	**c** Stroke whiskers across cheeks.	**d** Flap elbows like a waddling duck.

e Spread out hands behind ears and flap like elephant ears.	**f** Hold and direct imaginary hose towards fire.	**g** Mime holding a glass of grape juice in 'glug, glug' position.	**h** Breathe on to hand in front of mouth.

Letterland Early Years Handbook Published by Letterland International © Letterland International 2006

i Touch finger to thumb as if sticky and make an 'icky' face.

j Pretend to juggle an imaginary set of balls.

k Lift one arm and one foot in a **k**-shape.

l Touch finger tips above head to suggest Lucy's lamp-shade hat.

m Rub tummy and say 'mmm'.

n Bang one fist on the other, as if hammering a nail.

o Form round shapes with mouth and hand and look surprised.

p Stroke down long imaginary ears.

q Point index finger up as if ordering 'Quiet!'

r Make a running movement with arms.

s Make snake movements with hand and arm.

t Lift arms at shoulder height in a **t**-shape.

u Hold up imaginary umbrella with one hand low and the other above.

v Hold hands together in **v**-shape.

w Flick both hands up and away as if splashing water.

x Cross arms on chest in **x**-shape.

y Move hand up and down as if controlling a yo-yo.

z Tilt head and rest against hands to mime falling asleep.

Long vowel action

Each Vowel Man punches the air with his right hand as he calls out his name enthusiastically.

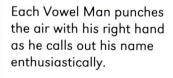

Letterland Early Years Handbook Published by Letterland International © Letterland International 2006

Dear Parent/Carer,

As part of our language teaching, we will be introducing your child's class to the alphabet using Letterland. This is a well-established and successful system for teaching children to read and write, and supports government curriculum guidelines and the Early Years Foundation Stage.

Letter shapes and sounds are abstract and often hard for children to learn. In Letterland, letters become friendly 'pictogram' characters. For example, the pictogram character for the letter a is Annie Apple.

Your child will learn about the characters which make up the Letterland alphabet. These characters will help your child to know and understand letter shapes and sounds. Don't be surprised if your child comes home full of talk about Annie Apple or Clever Cat. Show an interest in the characters, even if you don't understand what your child is talking about just yet!

Please help us in this adventure in the following ways:

- A letter name is quite different from the sound a letter makes, and only five of them (**a**, **e**, **i**, **o**, **u**) are ever used in reading. So try to avoid using the traditional 'aee', 'bee', 'cee' letter names at this stage. If your child already knows the alphabet names, just give them a rest for now. The Letterland character names are easier and more useful, so you might like to start using them yourself, too. When you talk about Clever Cat's letter, for instance, you can be sure to be understood, whereas children often confuse 'cee' with 'es'.

- We will be introducing both capital and small letters at the same time. However, in handwriting, please help us to emphasise the small letters first (**a**-z), since these are the most needed shapes. Use capital letters for the beginning of names only.

- Remember that holding the pencil correctly and forming letters in the right sequence is more important than neat writing at this stage.

Good relaxed grip

Poor tense grip

If you would like more information on using Letterland with your child, we will be happy to talk to you about it. You can also contact the publisher, Letterland International, at: **info@letterland.com** or visit: **www.letterland.com**.

We are looking forward to introducing your child to the world of Letterland and we hope you will join in the fun and the learning   with your child at home.

Thank you for your help.